Songs & Other Verse by Eugene Field

Eugene Field was born on 2nd September 1850 in St. Louis, Missouri. His mother died when he was six and his father when he was nineteen. His academic life was not taken seriously and he preferred the life of a prankster until, in 1875, he began work as a journalist for the St. Joseph Gazette in Saint Joseph, Missouri.

In his career as a journalist he soon found a niche that suited him. His articles were light, humorous and written in a personal gossipy style that endeared him to his readership. Some were soon being syndicated to other newspapers around the States. Field soon rose to city editor of the Gazette.

Field had first published poetry in 1879, when his poem 'Christmas Treasures' appeared. This was the beginning that would eventually number over a dozen volumes. As well as verse Field published an extensive range of short stories including 'The Holy Cross' and 'Daniel and the Devil.'

In 1889 whilst the family were in London and Field himself was recovering from a bout of ill health he wrote his most famous poem; 'Lovers Lane'.

On 4th November 1895 Eugene Field Sr died in Chicago of a heart attack at the age of 45.

Index of Contents

THE SINGING IN GOD'S ACRE
THE DREAM-SHIP
TO CINNA
BALLAD OF WOMEN I LOVE
SUPPOSE
MYSTERIOUS DOINGS
WITH TWO SPOONS FOR TWO SPOONS
MARY SMITH
JESSIE
TO EMMA ABBOTT
THE GREAT JOURNALIST IN SPAIN
LOVE SONG—HEINE
THE STODDARDS
THE THREE TAILORS
THE JAFFA AND JERUSALEM RAILWAY
HUGO'S "POOL IN THE FOREST"
A RHINE-LAND DRINKING SONG
DER MANN IM KELLER
TWO IDYLLS FROM BION THE SMYRNEAN
THE WOOING OF THE SOUTHLAND
HYMN
STAR OF THE EAST
TWIN IDOLS
TWO VALENTINES
MOTHER AND SPHINX
A SPRING POEM FROM BION
BÉRANGER'S "TO MY OLD COAT"
BEN APFELGARTEN

I0157403

A HEINE LOVE SONG
UHLAND'S "CHAPEL"
THE DREAMS
IN NEW ORLEANS
MY PLAYMATES
STOVES AND SUNSHINE
A DRINKING SONG
THE LIMITATIONS OF YOUTH
THE BOW-LEG BOY
THE STRAW PARLOR
A PITEOUS PLAINT
THE DISCREET COLLECTOR
A VALENTINE
THE WIND
A PARAPHRASE
WITH BRUTUS IN ST. JO
THE TWO LITTLE SKEEZUCKS
PAN LIVETH
DR. SAM
WINFREDA
LYMAN, FREDERICK, AND JIM
BE MY SWEETHEART
THE PETER-BIRD
SISTER'S CAKE
ABU MIDJAN
ED
JENNIE
CONTENTMENT
"GUESS"
NEW-YEAR'S EVE
OLD SPANISH SONG
THE BROKEN RING
IN PRAISE OF CONTENTMENT
THE BALLAD OF THE TAYLOR PUP
AFTER READING TROLLOPE'S HISTORY OF FLORENCE
A LULLABY
"THE OLD HOMESTEAD"
CHRISTMAS HYMN
A PARAPHRASE OF HEINE
THE CONVALESCENT GRIPSTER
THE SLEEPING CHILD
THE TWO COFFINS
CLARE MARKET
A DREAM OF SPRINGTIME
UHLAND'S WHITE STAG
HOW SALTY WIN OUT
EUGENE FIELD – A SHORT BIOGRAPHY
EUGENE FIELD – A CONCISE BIBILIOGRAPHY

THE SINGING IN GOD'S ACRE

Out yonder in the moonlight, wherein God's Acre lies,
Go angels walking to and fro, singing their lullabies.
Their radiant wings are folded, and their eyes are bended low,
As they sing among the beds whereon the flowers delight to grow,—

"Sleep, oh, sleep!
The Shepherd guardeth His sheep.
Fast speedeth the night away,
Soon cometh the glorious day;
Sleep, weary ones, while ye may,
Sleep, oh, sleep!"

The flowers within God's Acre see that fair and wondrous sight,
And hear the angels singing to the sleepers through the night;
And, lo! throughout the hours of day those gentle flowers prolong
The music of the angels in that tender slumber-song,—

"Sleep, oh, sleep!
The Shepherd loveth His sheep.
He that guardeth His flock the best
Hath folded them to His loving breast;
So sleep ye now, and take your rest,—
Sleep, oh, sleep!"

From angel and from flower the years have learned that soothing song,
And with its heavenly music speed the days and nights along;
So through all time, whose flight the Shepherd's vigils glorify,
God's Acre slumbereth in the grace of that sweet lullaby,—

"Sleep, oh, sleep!
The Shepherd loveth His sheep.
Fast speedeth the night away,
Soon cometh the glorious day;
Sleep, weary ones, while ye may,—
Sleep, oh, sleep!"

THE DREAM-SHIP

When the world is fast asleep,
Along the midnight skies—
As though it were a wandering cloud—
The ghostly dream-ship flies.

An angel stands at the dream-ship's helm,
An angel stands at the prow,
And an angel stands at the dream-ship's side
With a rue-wreath on her brow.

The other angels, silver-crowned,
Pilot and helmsman are,
And the angel with the wreath of rue
Tosseth the dreams afar.

The dreams they fall on rich and poor;
They fall on young and old;
And some are dreams of poverty,
And some are dreams of gold.

And some are dreams that thrill with joy,
And some that melt to tears;
Some are dreams of the dawn of love,
And some of the old dead years.

On rich and poor alike they fall,
Alike on young and old,
Bringing to slumbering earth their joys
And sorrows manifold.

The friendless youth in them shall do
The deeds of mighty men,
And drooping age shall feel the grace
Of buoyant youth again.

The king shall be a beggarman—
The pauper be a king—
In that revenge or recompense
The dream-ship dreams do bring.

So ever downward float the dreams
That are for all and me,
And there is never mortal man
Can solve that mystery.

But ever onward in its course
Along the haunted skies—
As though it were a cloud astray—
The ghostly dream-ship flies.

Two angels with their silver crowns
Pilot and helmsman are,
And an angel with a wreath of rue
Tosseth the dreams afar.

TO CINNA

Cinna, the great Venusian told

In songs that will not die
How in Augustan days of old
Your love did glorify
His life and all his being seemed
Thrilled by that rare incense
Till, grudging him the dreams he dreamed,
The gods did call you hence.

Cinna, I've looked into your eyes,
And held your hands in mine,
And seen your cheeks in sweet surprise
Blush red as Massic wine;
Now let the songs in Cinna's praise
Be chanted once again,
For, oh! alone I walk the ways
We walked together then!

Perhaps upon some star to-night,
So far away in space
I cannot see that beacon light
Nor feel its soothing grace—
Perhaps from that far-distant sphere
Her quickened vision seeks
For this poor heart of mine that here
To its lost Cinna speaks.

Then search this heart, beloved eyes,
And find it still as true
As when in all my boyhood skies
My guiding stars were you!
Cinna, you know the mystery
That is denied to men—
Mine is the lot to feel that we
Shall elsewhere love again!

BALLAD OF WOMEN I LOVE

Prudence Mears hath an old blue plate
Hid away in an oaken chest,
And a Franklin platter of ancient date
Beareth Amandy Baker's crest;
What times soever I've been their guest,
Says I to myself in an undertone:
"Of womenfolk, it must be confessed,
These do I love, and these alone."

Well, again, in the Nutmeg State,
Dorothy Pratt is richly blest
With a relic of art and a land effete—

A pitcher of glass that's cut, not pressed.
And a Washington teapot is possessed
Down in Pelham by Marthy Stone—
Think ye now that I say in jest
"These do I love, and these alone?"

Were Hepsy Higgins inclined to mate,
Or Dorcas Eastman prone to invest
In Cupid's bonds, they could find their fate
In the bootless bard of Crockery Quest.
For they've heaps of trumpery—so have the rest
Of those spinsters whose ware I'd like to own;
You can see why I say with such certain zest,
"These do I love, and these alone."

ENVOY

Prince, show me the quickest way and best
To gain the subject of my moan;
We've neither spinsters nor relics out West—
These do I love, and these alone.

SUPPOSE

Suppose, my dear, that you were I
And by your side your sweetheart sate;
Suppose you noticed by and by
The distance 'twixt you were too great;
Now tell me, dear, what would you do?
I know—and so do you.

And when (so comfortably placed)
Suppose you only grew aware
That that dear, dainty little waist
Of hers looked very lonely there;
Pray tell me sooth—what would you do?
I know, and so do you.

When, having done what I just did
With not a frown to check or chill,
Suppose her red lips seemed to bid
Defiance to your lordly will;
Oh, tell me, sweet, what would you do?
I know, and so do you.

MYSTERIOUS DOINGS

As once I rambled in the woods
I chanced to spy amid the brake
A huntsman ride his way beside
A fair and passing tranquil lake;
Though velvet bucks sped here and there,
He let them scamper through the green—
Not one smote he, but lustily
He blew his horn—what could it mean?

As on I strolled beside that lake,
A pretty maid I chanced to see
Fishing away for finny prey,
Yet not a single one caught she;
All round her boat the fishes leapt
And gambolled to their hearts' content,
Yet never a thing did the maid but sing—
I wonder what on earth it meant.

As later yet I roamed my way,
A lovely steed neighed loud and long,
And an empty boat sped all afloat
Where sang a fishermaid her song;
All underneath the prudent shade,
Which yonder kindly willows threw,
Together strayed a youth and maid—
I can't explain it all, can you?

WITH TWO SPOONS FOR TWO SPOONS

How trifling shall these gifts appear
Among the splendid many
That loving friends now send to cheer
Harvey and Ellen Jenney.

And yet these baubles symbolize
A certain fond relation
That well beseems, as I surmise,
This festive celebration.

Sweet friends of mine, be spoons once more,
And with your tender cooing
Renew the keen delights of yore—
The rapturous bliss of wooing.

What though that silver in your hair
Tells of the years aflying?
'T is yours to mock at Time and Care
With love that is undying.

In memory of this Day, dear friends,
Accept the modest token
From one who with the bauble sends
A love that can't be spoken.

MARY SMITH

Away down East where I was reared amongst my Yankee kith,
There used to live a pretty girl whose name was Mary Smith;
And though it's many years since last I saw that pretty girl,
And though I feel I'm sadly worn by Western strife and whirl;
Still, oftentimes, I think about the old familiar place,
Which, someway, seemed the brighter for Miss Mary's pretty face,
And in my heart I feel once more revivified the glow
I used to feel in those old times when I was Mary's beau.

I saw her home from singing school—she warbled like a bird.
A sweeter voice than hers for song or speech I never heard.
She was soprano in the choir, and I a solemn bass,
And when we unisoned our voices filled that holy place;
The tenor and the alto never had the slightest chance,
For Mary's upper register made every heart-string dance;
And, as for me, I shall not brag, and yet I'd have you know
I sung a very likely bass when I was Mary's beau.

On Friday nights I'd drop around to make my weekly call,
And though I came to visit her, I'd have to see 'em all.
With Mary's mother sitting here and Mary's father there,
The conversation never flagged so far as I'm aware;
Sometimes I'd hold her worsted, sometimes we'd play at games,
Sometimes dissect the apples which we'd named each other's names.
Oh how I loathed the shrill-toned clock that told me when to go—
'Twas ten o'clock at half-past eight when I was Mary's beau.

Now there was Luther Baker—because he'd come of age
And thought himself some pumpkins because he drove the stage—
He fancied he could cut me out; but Mary was my friend—
Elsewise I'm sure the issue had had a tragic end.
For Luther Baker was a man I never could abide,
And, when it came to Mary, either he or I had died.
I merely cite this instance incidentally to show
That I was quite in earnest when I was Mary's beau.

How often now those sights, those pleasant sights, recur again:
The little township that was all the world I knew of then—
The meeting-house upon the hill, the tavern just beyond,
Old deacon Packard's general store, the sawmill by the pond,
The village elms I vainly sought to conquer in my quest
Of that surpassing trophy, the golden oriole's nest.

And, last of all those visions that come back from long ago,
The pretty face that thrilled my soul when I was Mary's beau.

Hush, gentle wife, there is no need a pang should vex your heart—
'T is many years since fate ordained that she and I should part;
To each a true, maturer love came in good time, and yet
It brought not with its nobler grace the power to forget.
And would you fain begrudge me now the sentimental joy
That comes of recollections of my sparkings when a boy?
I warrant me that, were your heart put to the rack, 't would show
That it had predilections when I was Mary's beau.

And, Mary, should these lines of mine seek out your biding place,
God grant they bring the old sweet smile back to your pretty face—
God grant they bring you thoughts of me, not as I am to-day,
With faltering step and brimming eyes and aspect grimly gray;
But thoughts that picture me as fair and full of life and glee
As we were in the olden times—as you shall always be.
Think of me ever, Mary, as the boy you used to know
When time was fleet, and life was sweet, and I was Mary's beau.

Dear hills of old New England, look down with tender eyes
Upon one little lonely grave that in your bosom lies;
For in that cradle sleeps a child who was so fair to see
God yearned to have unto Himself the joy she brought to me;
And bid your winds sing soft and low the song of other days,
When, hand in hand and heart to heart, we went our pleasant ways—
Ah me! but could I sing again that song of long ago,
Instead of this poor idle song of being Mary's beau.

JESSIE

When I remark her golden hair
Swoon on her glorious shoulders,
I marvel not that sight so rare
Doth ravish all beholders;
For summon hence all pretty girls
Renowned for beauteous tresses,
And you shall find among their curls
There's none so fair as Jessie's.

And Jessie's eyes are, oh, so blue
And full of sweet revealings—
They seem to look you through and through
And read your inmost feelings;
Nor black emits such ardent fires,
Nor brown such truth expresses—
Admit it, all ye gallant squires—
There are no eyes like Jessie's.

Her voice (like liquid beams that roll
From moonland to the river)
Steals subtly to the raptured soul,
Therein to lie and quiver;
Or falls upon the grateful ear
With chaste and warm caresses—
Ah, all concede the truth (who hear):
There's no such voice as Jessie's.

Of other charms she hath such store
All rivalry excelling,
Though I used adjectives galore,
They'd fail me in the telling;
But now discretion stays my hand—
Adieu, eyes, voice, and tresses.
Of all the husbands in the land
There's none so fierce as Jessie's.

TO EMMA ABBOTT

There—let thy hands be folded
Awhile in sleep's repose;
The patient hands that wearied not,
But earnestly and nobly wrought
In charity and faith;
And let thy dear eyes close—
The eyes that looked alway to God,
Nor quailed beneath the chastening rod
Of sorrow;
Fold thou thy hands and eyes
For just a little while,
And with a smile
Dream of the morrow.

And, O white voiceless flower,
The dream which thou shalt dream
Should be a glimpse of heavenly things,
For yonder like a seraph sings
The sweetness of a life
With faith alway its theme;
While speedeth from those realms above
The messenger of that dear love
That healeth sorrow.
So sleep a little while,
For thou shalt wake and sing
Before thy King
When cometh the morrow.

THE GREAT JOURNALIST IN SPAIN

Good editor Dana—God bless him, we say—
Will soon be afloat on the main,
Will be steaming away
Through the mist and the spray
To the sensuous climate of Spain.

Strange sights shall he see in that beautiful land
Which is famed for its soap and its Moor,
For, as we understand,
The scenery is grand
Though the system of railways is poor.

For moonlight of silver and sunlight of gold
Glint the orchards of lemons and mangoes,
And the ladies, we're told,
Are a joy to behold
As they twine in their lissome fandangoes.

What though our friend Dana shall twang a guitar
And murmur a passionate strain;
Oh, fairer by far
Than those ravishments are
The castles abounding in Spain.

These castles are built as the builder may list—
They are sometimes of marble or stone,
But they mostly consist
Of east wind and mist
With an ivy of froth overgrown.

A beautiful castle our Dana shall raise
On a futile foundation of hope,
And its glories shall blaze
In the somnolent haze
Of the mythical lake del y Soap.

The fragrance of sunflowers shall swoon on the air
And the visions of Dreamland obtain,
And the song of "World's Fair"
Shall be heard everywhere
Through that beautiful castle in Spain.

LOVE SONG—HEINE

Many a beauteous flower doth spring

From the tears that flood my eyes,
And the nightingale doth sing
In the burthen of my sighs.

If, O child, thou lovest me,
Take these flowerets fair and frail,
And my soul shall waft to thee
Love songs of the nightingale.

THE STODDARDS

When I am in New York, I like to drop around at night,
To visit with my honest, genial friends, the Stoddards hight;
Their home in Fifteenth street is all so snug, and furnished so,
That, when I once get planted there, I don't know when to go;
A cosy cheerful refuge for the weary homesick guest,
Combining Yankee comforts with the freedom of the west.

The first thing you discover, as you maunder through the hall,
Is a curious little clock upon a bracket on the wall;
'T was made by Stoddard's father, and it's very, very old—
The connoisseurs assure me it is worth its weight in gold;
And I, who've bought all kinds of clocks, 'twixt Denver and the Rhine,
Cast envious eyes upon that clock, and wish that it were mine.

But in the parlor. Oh, the gems on tables, walls, and floor—
Rare first editions, etchings, and old crockery galore.
Why, talk about the Indies and the wealth of Orient things—
They couldn't hold a candle to these quaint and sumptuous things;
In such profusion, too—Ah me! how dearly I recall
How I have sat and watched 'em and wished I had 'em all.

Now, Mr. Stoddard's study is on the second floor,
A wee blind dog barks at me as I enter through the door;
The Cerberus would fain begrudge what sights it cannot see,
The rapture of that visual feast it cannot share with me;
A miniature edition this—this most absurd of hounds—
A genuine unique, I'm sure, and one unknown to Lowndes.

Books—always books—are piled around; some musty, and all old;
Tall, solemn folios such as Lamb declared he loved to hold;
Large paper copies with their virgin margins white and wide,
And presentation volumes with the author's comps. inside;
I break the tenth commandment with a wild impassioned cry:
Oh, how came Stoddard by these things? Why Stoddard, and not I?

From yonder wall looks Thackeray upon his poet friend,
And underneath the genial face appear the lines he penned;
And here, gadzooks, ben honge ye prynte of marvaillous renowne

Yt shameth Chaucers gallaunt knyghtes in Canterbury towne;
And still more books and pictures. I'm dazed, bewildered, vexed;
Since I've broke the tenth commandment, why not break the eighth one next?

And, furthermore, in confidence inviolate be it said
Friend Stoddard owns a lock of hair that grew on Milton's head;
Now I have Gladstone axes and a lot of curious things,
Such as pimply Dresden teacups and old German wedding-rings;
But nothing like that saintly lock have I on wall or shelf,
And, being somewhat short of hair, I should like that lock myself.

But Stoddard has a soothing way, as though he grieved to see
Invidious torments prey upon a nice young chap like me.
He waves me to an easy chair and hands me out a weed
And pumps me full of that advice he seems to know I need;
So sweet the tap of his philosophy and knowledge flows
That I can't help wishing that I knew a half what Stoddard knows.

And so we sit for hours and hours, praising without restraint
The people who are thoroughbreds, and roasting the ones that ain't;
Happy, thrice happy, is the man we happen to admire,
But wretched, oh, how wretched he that hath provoked our ire;
For I speak emphatic English when I once get fairly r'iled,
And Stoddard's wrath's an Ossa upon a Pelion piled.

Out yonder, in the alcove, a lady sits and darns,
And interjects remarks that always serve to spice our yarns;
She's Mrs. Stoddard; there's a dame that's truly to my heart:
A tiny little woman, but so quaint, and good, and smart
That, if you asked me to suggest which one I should prefer
Of all the Stoddard treasures, I should promptly mention her.

O dear old man, how I should like to be with you this night,
Down in your home in Fifteenth street, where all is snug and bright;
Where the shaggy little Cerberus dreams in its cushioned place,
And the books and pictures all around smile in their old friend's face;
Where the dainty little sweetheart, whom you still were proud to woo,
Charms back the tender memories so dear to her and you.

THE THREE TAILORS

I shall tell you in rhyme how, once on a time,
Three tailors tramped up to the inn Ingleheim,
On the Rhine, lovely Rhine;
They were broke, but the worst of it all, they were curst
With that malady common to tailors—a thirst
For wine, lots of wine.

"Sweet host," quoth the three, "we're hard up as can be,

Yet skilled in the practice of cunning are we,
On the Rhine, genial Rhine;
And we pledge you we will impart you that skill
Right quickly and fully, providing you'll fill
Us with wine, cooling wine."

But that host shook his head, and he warily said:
"Though cunning be good, we take money instead,
On the Rhine, thrifty Rhine;
If ye fancy ye may without pelf have your way
You'll find that there's both host and the devil to pay
For your wine, costly wine."

Then the first knavish wight took his needle so bright
And threaded its eye with a wee ray of light
From the Rhine, sunny Rhine;
And, in such a deft way, patched a mirror that day
That where it was mended no expert could say—
Done so fine 't was for wine.

The second thereat spied a poor little gnat
Go toiling along on his nose broad and flat
Towards the Rhine, pleasant Rhine;
"Aha, tiny friend, I should hate to offend,
But your stockings need darning"—which same did he mend,
All for wine, soothing wine.

And next there occurred what you'll deem quite absurd—
His needle a space in the wall thrust the third,
By the Rhine, wondrous Rhine;
And then all so spry, he leapt through the eye
Of that thin cambric needle—nay, think you I'd lie
About wine—not for wine.

The landlord allowed (with a smile) he was proud
To do the fair thing by that talented crowd
On the Rhine, generous Rhine.
So a thimble filled he as full as could be—
"Drink long and drink hearty, my jolly friends three,
Of my wine, filling wine."

THE JAFFA AND JERUSALEM RAILWAY

A tortuous double iron track; a station here, a station there;
A locomotive, tender, tanks; a coach with stiff reclining chair;
Some postal cars, and baggage, too; a vestibule of patent make;
With buffers, duffers, switches, and the soughing automatic brake—
This is the Orient's novel pride, and Syria's gaudiest modern gem:
The railway scheme that is to ply 'twixt Jaffa and Jerusalem.

Beware, O sacred Mooley cow, the engine when you hear its bell;
Beware, O camel, when resounds the whistle's shrill, unholy swell;
And, native of that guileless land, unused to modern travel's snare,
Beware the fiend that peddles books—the awful peanut-boy beware.
Else, trusting in their specious arts, you may have reason to condemn
The traffic which the knavish ply 'twixt Jaffa and Jerusalem.

And when, ah, when the bonds fall due, how passing wroth will wax the state
From Nebo's mount to Nazareth will spread the cry "Repudiate"!
From Hebron to Tiberius, from Jordan's banks unto the sea,
Will rise profuse anathemas against "that — monopoly!"
And F.M.B.A. shepherd-folk, with Sockless Jerry leading them,
Will swamp that corporation line 'twixt Jaffa and Jerusalem.

HUGO'S "POOL IN THE FOREST"

How calm, how beauteous and how cool—
How like a sister to the skies,
Appears the broad, transparent pool
That in this quiet forest lies.
The sunshine ripples on its face,
And from the world around, above,
It hath caught down the nameless grace
Of such reflections as we love.

But deep below its surface crawl
The reptile horrors of the night—
The dragons, lizards, serpents—all
The hideous brood that hate the light;
Through poison fern and slimy weed
And under ragged, jagged stones
They scuttle, or, in ghoulish greed,
They lap a dead man's bleaching bones.

And as, O pool, thou dost cajole
With seemings that beguile us well,
So doeth many a human soul
That teemeth with the lusts of hell.

A RHINE-LAND DRINKING SONG

If our own life is the life of a flower
(And that's what some sages are thinking),
We should moisten the bud with a health-giving flood
And 'twill bloom all the sweeter—
Yes, life's the completer

For drinking,
and drinking,
and drinking.

If it be that our life is a journey
(As many wise folk are opining),
We should sprinkle the way with the rain while we may;
Though dusty and dreary,
'Tis made cool and cheery
With wining,
and wining,
and wining.

If this life that we live be a dreaming
(As pessimist people are thinking),
To induce pleasant dreams there is nothing, meseems,
Like this sweet prescription,
That baffles description—
This drinking,
and drinking,
and drinking.

DER MANN IM KELLER

How cool and fair this cellar where
My throne a dusky cask is;
To do no thing but just to sing
And drown the time my task is.
The cooper he's
Resolved to please,
And, answering to my winking,
He fills me up
Cup after cup
For drinking, drinking, drinking.

Begrudge me not
This cosy spot
In which I am reclining—
Why, who would burst
With envious thirst,
When he can live by wining.
A roseate hue seems to imbue
The world on which I'm blinking;
My fellow-men—I love them when
I'm drinking, drinking, drinking.

And yet I think, the more I drink,
It's more and more I pine for—
Oh, such as I (forever dry)

God made this land of Rhine for;
And there is bliss
In knowing this,
As to the floor I'm sinking:
I've wronged no man
And never can
While drinking, drinking, drinking.

TWO IDYLLS FROM BION THE SMYRNEAN

I

Once a fowler, young and artless,
To the quiet greenwood came;
Full of skill was he and heartless
In pursuit of feathered game.
And betimes he chanced to see
Eros perching in a tree.

"What strange bird is that, I wonder?"
Thought the youth, and spread his snare;
Eros, chuckling at the blunder,
Gayly scampered here and there.
Do his best, the simple clod
Could not snare the agile god!

Blubbering, to his aged master
Went the fowler in dismay,
And confided his disaster
With that curious bird that day;
"Master, hast thou ever heard
Of so ill-disposed a bird?"

"Heard of him? Aha, most truly!"
Quoth the master with a smile;
"And thou too, shall know him duly—
Thou art young, but bide awhile,
And old Eros will not fly
From thy presence by and by!

"For when thou art somewhat older
That same Eros thou didst see,
More familiar grown and bolder,
Shall become acquaint with thee;
And when Eros comes thy way
Mark my word, he comes to stay!"

II

Once came Venus to me, bringing
Eros where my cattle fed—
"Teach this little boy your singing,
Gentle herdsman," Venus said.
I was young—I did not know
Whom it was that Venus led—
That was many years ago!

In a lusty voice but mellow—
Callow pedant! I began
To instruct the little fellow
In the mysteries known to man;
Sung the noble cithern's praise,
And the flute of dear old Pan,
And the lyre that Hermes plays.

But he paid no heed unto me—
Nay, that graceless little boy
Coolly plotted to undo me—
With his songs of tender joy;
And my pedantry o'erthrown,
Eager was I to employ
His sweet ritual for mine own!

Ah, these years of ours are fleeting!
Yet I have not vainly wrought,
Since to-day I am repeating
What dear lessons Eros taught;
Love, and always love, and then—
Counting all things else for naught—
Love and always love again!

THE WOOING OF THE SOUTHLAND

(ALASKAN BALLAD)

The Northland reared his hoary head
And spied the Southland leagues away—
"Fairest of all fair brides," he said,
"Be thou my bride, I pray!"

Whereat the Southland laughed and cried:
"I'll bide beside my native sea,
And I shall never be thy bride
Till thou com'st wooing me!"

The Northland's heart was a heart of ice,
A diamond glacier, mountain high—

Oh, love is sweet at any price,
As well know you and I!

So gayly the Northland took his heart
And cast it in the wailing sea—
"Go, thou, with all thy cunning art,
And woo my bride for me!"

For many a night and for many a day,
And over the leagues that rolled between,
The true-heart messenger sped away
To woo the Southland queen.

But the sea wailed loud, and the sea wailed long,
While ever the Northland cried in glee:
"Oh, thou shalt sing us our bridal song,
When comes my bride, O sea!"

At the foot of the Southland's golden throne
The heart of the Northland ever throbs—
For that true-heart speaks in the waves that moan,
The songs that it sings are sobs.

Ever the Southland spurns the cries
Of the messenger pleading the Northland's part;
The summer shines in the Southland's eyes—
The winter bides in her heart!

And ever unto that far-off place
Which love doth render a hallowed spot,
The Northland turneth his honest face
And wonders she cometh not.

The sea wails loud, and the sea wails long,
As the ages of waiting drift slowly by,
But the sea shall sing no bridal song—
As well know you and I!

HYMN

(FROM THE GERMAN OF MARTIN LUTHER)

O heart of mine! lift up thine eyes
And see who in yon manger lies!
Of perfect form, of face divine—
It is the Christ-child, heart of mine!

O dearest, holiest Christ-child, spread
Within this heart of mine thy bed;

Then shall my breast forever be
A chamber consecrate to thee!

Beat high to-day, O heart of mine,
And tell, O lips, what joys are thine;
For with your help shall I prolong
Old Bethlehem's sweetest cradle-song.

Glory to God, whom this dear Child
Hath by His coming reconciled,
And whose redeeming love again
Brings peace on earth, good will to men!

STAR OF THE EAST

Star of the East, that long ago
Brought wise men on their way
Where, angels singing to and fro,
The Child of Bethlehem lay—
Above that Syrian hill afar
Thou shinest out to-night, O Star!

Star of the East, the night were drear
But for the tender grace
That with thy glory comes to cheer
Earth's loneliest, darkest place;
For by that charity we see
Where there is hope for all and me.

Star of the East! show us the way
In wisdom undefiled
To seek that manger out and lay
Our gifts before the child—
To bring our hearts and offer them
Unto our King in Bethlehem!

TWIN IDOLS

There are two phrases, you must know,
So potent (yet so small)
That wheresoe'er a man may go
He needs none else at all;
No servile guide to lead the way
Nor lackey at his heel,
If he be learned enough to say
"Comme bien" and "Wie viel."

The sleek, pomaded Parleyvoo
Will air his sweetest airs
And quote the highest rates when you
"Comme bien" for his wares;
And, though the German stolid be,
His so-called heart of steel
Becomes as soft as wax when he
Detects the words "Wie viel."

Go, search the boulevards and rues
From Havre to Marseilles—
You'll find all eloquence you use
Except "Comme bien" fails;
Or in the country auf der Rhine
Essay a business deal
And all your art is good fuhr nein
Beyond the point—"Wie viel."

It matters not what game or prey
Attracts your greedy eyes—
You must pursue the good old way
If you would win the prize;
It is to get a titled mate
All run down at the heel,
If you inquire of stock effete,
"Comme bien" or "Wie viel."

So he is wise who envieth not
A wealth of foreign speech,
Since with two phrases may be got
Whatever's in his reach;
For Europe is a soulless shrine
In which all classes kneel
Before twin idols, deemed divine—
"Comme bien" and "Wie viel."

TWO VALENTINES

I.—TO MISTRESS BARBARA

There were three cavaliers, all handsome and true,
On Valentine's day came a maiden to woo,
And quoth to your mother: "Good-morrow, my dear,
We came with some songs for your daughter to hear!"

Your mother replied: "I'll be pleased to convey
To my daughter what things you may sing or may say!"

Then the first cavalier sung: "My pretty red rose,

I'll love you and court you some day, I suppose!"

And the next cavalier sung, with make-believe tears:
"I've loved you! I've loved you these many long years!"

But the third cavalier (with the brown, bushy head
And the pretty blue jacket and necktie of red)
He drew himself up with a resolute air,
And he warbled: "O maiden, surpassingly fair!
I've loved you long years, and I love you to-day,
And, if you will let me, I'll love you for aye!"

I (the third cavalier) sang this ditty to you,
In my necktie of red and my jacket of blue;
I'm sure you'll prefer the song that was mine
And smile your approval on your valentine.

II.—TO A BABY BOY

Who I am I shall not say,
But I send you this bouquet
With this query, baby mine:
"Will you be my valentine?"

See these roses blushing blue,
Very like your eyes of hue;
While these violets are the red
Of your cheeks. It can be said
Ne'er before was babe like you.

And I think it is quite true
No one e'er before to-day
Sent so wondrous a bouquet
As these posies aforesaid—
Roses blue and violets red!

Sweet, repay me sweets for sweets—
'Tis your lover who entreats!
Smile upon me, baby mine—
Be my little valentine!

MOTHER AND SPHINX

(EGYPTIAN FOLK-SONG)

Grim is the face that looks into the night
Over the stretch of sands;
A sullen rock in a sea of white—

A ghostly shadow in ghostly light,
Peering and moaning it stands.
"Oh, is it the king that rides this way—
Oh, is it the king that rides so free?
I have looked for the king this many a day,
But the years that mock me will not say
Why tarrieth he!"

'T is not your king that shall ride to-night,
But a child that is fast asleep;
And the horse he shall ride is the Dream-horse white—
Aha, he shall speed through the ghostly light
Where the ghostly shadows creep!
"My eyes are dull and my face is sere,
Yet unto the word he gave I cling,
For he was a Pharaoh that set me here—
And, lo! I have waited this many a year
For him—my king!"

Oh, past thy face my darling shall ride
Swift as the burning winds that bear
The sand clouds over the desert wide—
Swift to the verdure and palms beside
The wells off there!
"And is it the mighty king I shall see
Come riding into the night?
Oh, is it the king come back to me—
Proudly and fiercely rideth he,
With centuries dight!"

I know no king but my dark-eyed dear
That shall ride the Dream-Horse white;
But see! he wakes at my bosom here,
While the Dream-Horse frettingly lingers near
To speed with my babe to-night!
And out of the desert darkness peers
A ghostly, ghastly, shadowy thing
Like a spirit come out of the mouldering years,
And ever that waiting spectre hears
The coming king!

A SPRING POEM FROM BION

One asketh:
"Tell me, Myrson, tell me true:
What's the season pleaseth you?
Is it summer suits you best,
When from harvest toil we rest?
Is it autumn with its glory

Of all surfeited desires?
Is it winter, when with story
And with song we hug our fires?
Or is spring most fair to you—
Come, good Myrson, tell me true!"

Another answereth:
"What the gods in wisdom send
We should question not, my friend;
Yet, since you entreat of me,
I will answer reverently:
Me the summertime displeases,
For its sun is scorching hot;
Autumn brings such dire diseases
That perforce I like it not;
As for biting winter, oh!
How I hate its ice and snow!

"But, thrice welcome, kindly spring,
With the myriad gifts you bring!
Not too hot nor yet too cold,
Graciously your charms unfold—
Oh, your days are like the dreaming
Of those nights which love beseems,
And your nights have all the seeming
Of those days of golden dreams!
Heaven smiles down on earth, and then
Earth smiles up to heaven again!"

BÉRANGER'S "TO MY OLD COAT."

Still serve me in my age, I pray,
As in my youth, O faithful one;
For years I've brushed thee every day—
Could Socrates have better done?
What though the fates would wreak on thee
The fulness of their evil art?
Use thou philosophy, like me—
And we, old friend, shall never part!

I think—I often think of it—
The day we twain first faced the crowd;
My roistering friends impeached your fit,
But you and I were very proud!
Those jovial friends no more make free
With us (no longer new and smart),
But rather welcome you and me
As loving friends that should not part.

The patch? Oh, yes—one happy night—
"Lisette," says I, "it's time to go"—
She clutched this sleeve to stay my flight,
Shrieking: "What! leave so early? No!"
To mend the ghastly rent she'd made,
Three days she toiled, dear patient heart!
And I—right willingly I staid—
Lisette decreed we should not part!

No incense ever yet profaned
This honest, shiny warp of thine,
Nor hath a courtier's eye disdained
Thy faded hue and quaint design;
Let servile flattery be the price
Of ribbons in the royal mart—
A roadside posie shall suffice
For us two friends that must not part!

Fear not the recklessness of yore
Shall re-occur to vex thee now;
Alas, I am a youth no more—
I'm old and sere, and so art thou!
So bide with me unto the last
And with thy warmth caress this heart
That pleads, by memories of the Past,
That two such friends should never part!

BEN APFELGARTEN

There was a certain gentleman, Ben Apfelgarten called,
Who lived way off in Germany a many years ago,
And he was very fortunate in being very bald
And so was very happy he was so.
He warbled all the day
Such songs as only they
Who are very, very circumspect and very happy may;
The people wondered why,
As the years went gliding by,
They never heard him once complain or even heave a sigh!

The women of the province fell in love with genial Ben,
Till (may be you can fancy it) the dickens was to pay
Among the callow students and the sober-minded men—
With the women-folk a-cuttin' up that way!
Why, they gave him turbans red
To adorn his hairless head,
And knitted jaunty nightcaps to protect him when abed!
In vain the rest demurred—
Not a single chiding word

Those ladies deigned to tolerate—remonstrance was absurd!

Things finally got into such a very dreadful way
That the others (oh, how artful) formed the politic design
To send him to the reichstag; so, one dull November day,
They elected him a member from the Rhine!
Then the other members said:
"Gott im Himmel! what a head!"
But they marvelled when his speeches they listened to or read;
And presently they cried:
"There must be heaps inside
Of the smooth and shiny cranium his constituents deride!"

Well, when at last he up 'nd died—long past his ninetieth year—
The strangest and the most lugubrious funeral he had,
For women came in multitudes to weep upon his bier—
The men all wond'ring why on earth the women had gone mad!
And this wonderment increased
Till the sympathetic priest
Inquired of those same ladies: "Why this fuss about deceased?"
Whereupon were they appalled,
For, as one, those women squalled:
"We doted on deceased for being bald—bald—bald!"

He was bald because his genius burnt that shock of hair away
Which, elsewise, clogs one's keenness and activity of mind;
And (barring present company, of course) I'm free to say
That, after all, it's intellect that captures womankind.
At any rate, since then
(With a precedent in Ben),
The women-folk have been in love with us bald-headed men!

A HEINE LOVE SONG

The image of the moon at night
All trembling in the ocean lies,
But she, with calm and steadfast light,
Moves proudly through the radiant skies,

How like the tranquil moon thou art—
Thou fairest flower of womankind!
And, look, within my fluttering heart
Thy image trembling is enshrined!

UHLAND'S "CHAPEL"

Yonder stands the hillside chapel

Mid the evergreens and rocks,
All day long it hears the song
Of the shepherd to his flocks.

Then the chapel bell goes tolling—
Knelling for a soul that's sped;
Silent and sad the shepherd lad
Hears the requiem for the dead.

Shepherd, singers of the valley,
Voiceless now, speed on before;
Soon shall knell that chapel bell
For the songs you'll sing no more.

THE DREAMS

Two dreams came down to earth one night
From the realm of mist and dew;
One was a dream of the old, old days,
And one was a dream of the new.

One was a dream of a shady lane
That led to the pickerel pond
Where the willows and rushes bowed themselves
To the brown old hills beyond.

And the people that peopled the old-time dream
Were pleasant and fair to see,
And the dreamer he walked with them again
As often of old walked he.

Oh, cool was the wind in the shady lane
That tangled his curly hair!
Oh, sweet was the music the robins made
To the springtime everywhere!

Was it the dew the dream had brought
From yonder midnight skies,
Or was it tears from the dear, dead years
That lay in the dreamer's eyes?

The other dream ran fast and free,
As the moon benignly shed
Her golden grace on the smiling face
In the little trundle-bed.

For 't was a dream of times to come—
Of the glorious noon of day—
Of the summer that follows the careless spring

When the child is done with play.

And 't was a dream of the busy world
Where valorous deeds are done;
Of battles fought in the cause of right,
And of victories nobly won.

It breathed no breath of the dear old home
And the quiet joys of youth;
It gave no glimpse of the good old friends
Or the old-time faith and truth.

But 't was a dream of youthful hopes,
And fast and free it ran,
And it told to a little sleeping child
Of a boy become a man!

These were the dreams that came one night
To earth from yonder sky;
These were the dreams two dreamers dreamed—
My little boy and I.

And in our hearts my boy and I
Were glad that it was so;
He loved to dream of days to come,
And I of long ago.

So from our dreams my boy and I
Unwillingly awoke,
But neither of his precious dream
Unto the other spoke.

Yet of the love we bore those dreams
Gave each his tender sign;
For there was triumph in his eyes—
And there were tears in mine!

IN NEW ORLEANS

'Twas in the Crescent City not long ago befell
The tear-compelling incident I now propose to tell;
So come, my sweet collector friends, and listen while I sing
Unto your delectation this brief, pathetic thing—
No lyric pitched in vaunting key, but just a requiem
Of blowing twenty dollars in by nine o'clock a.m.

Let critic folk the poet's use of vulgar slang upbraid,
But, when I'm speaking by the card, I call a spade a spade;
And I, who have been touched of that same mania, myself,

Am well aware that, when it comes to parting with his pelf,
The curio collector is so blindly lost in sin
That he doesn't spend his money—he simply blows it in!

In Royal street (near Conti) there's a lovely curio-shop,
And there, one balmy, fateful morn, it was my chance to stop;
To stop was hesitation—in a moment I was lost—
That kind of hesitation does not hesitate at cost!
I spied a pewter tankard there, and, my! it was a gem—
And the clock in old St. Louis told the hour of eight a.m.!

Three quaint Bohemian bottles, too, of yellow and of green,
Cut in archaic fashion that I ne'er before had seen;
A lovely, hideous platter wreathed about with pink and rose,
With its curious depression into which the gravy flows;
Two dainty silver salts—oh, there was no resisting them—
And I'd blown in twenty dollars by nine o'clock a.m.

With twenty dollars, one who is a prudent man, indeed,
Can buy the wealth of useful things his wife and children need;
Shoes, stockings, knickerbockers, gloves, bibs, nursing-bottles, caps,
A gown—the gown for which his spouse too long has pined, perhaps!
These and ten thousand other spectres harrow and condemn
The man who's blown in twenty by nine o'clock a.m.

Oh, mean advantage conscience takes (and one that I abhor!)
In asking one this question: "What did you buy it for?"
Why doesn't conscience ply its blessed trade before the act,
Before one's cussedness becomes a bald, accomplished fact—
Before one's fallen victim to the Tempter's stratagem
And blown in twenty dollars by nine o'clock a.m.?

Ah me! now that the deed is done, how penitent I am!
I was a roaring lion—behold a bleating lamb!
I've packed and shipped those precious things to that more precious wife
Who shares with our sweet babes the strange vicissitudes of life,
While he who, in his folly, gave up his store of wealth
Is far away, and means to keep his distance—for his health!

MY PLAYMATES

The wind comes whispering to me of the country green and cool—
Of redwing blackbirds chattering beside a reedy pool;
It brings me soothing fancies of the homestead on the hill,
And I hear the thrush's evening song and the robin's morning trill;
So I fall to thinking tenderly of those I used to know
Where the sassafras and snakeroot and checkerberries grow.

What has become of Ezra Marsh, who lived on Baker's hill?

And what's become of Noble Pratt, whose father kept the mill?
And what's become of Lizzie Crum and Anastasia Snell,
And of Roxie Root, who 'tended school in Boston for a spell?
They were the boys and they the girls who shared my youthful play—
They do not answer to my call! My playmates—where are they?

What has become of Levi and his little brother Joe,
Who lived next door to where we lived some forty years ago?
I'd like to see the Newton boys and Quincy Adams Brown,
And Hepsy Hall and Ella Cowles, who spelled the whole school down!
And Gracie Smith, the Cutler boys, Leander Snow, and all
Who I am sure would answer could they only hear my call!

I'd like to see Bill Warner and the Conkey boys again
And talk about the times we used to wish that we were men!
And one—I shall not name her—could I see her gentle face
And hear her girlish treble in this distant, lonely place!
The flowers and hopes of springtime—they perished long ago,
And the garden where they blossomed is white with winter snow.

O cottage 'neath the maples, have you seen those girls and boys
That but a little while ago made, oh! such pleasant noise?
O trees, and hills, and brooks, and lanes, and meadows, do you know
Where I shall find my little friends of forty years ago?
You see I'm old and weary, and I've traveled long and far;
I am looking for my playmates—I wonder where they are!

STOVES AND SUNSHINE

Prate, ye who will, of so-called charms you find across the sea—
The land of stoves and sunshine is good enough for me!
I've done the grand for fourteen months in every foreign clime,
And I've learned a heap of learning, but I've shivered all the time;
And the biggest bit of wisdom I've acquired—as I can see—
Is that which teaches that this land's the land of lands for me.

Now, I am of opinion that a person should get some
Warmth in this present life of ours, not all in that to come;
So when Boreas blows his blast, through country and through town,
Or when upon the muddy streets the stifling fog rolls down,
Go, guzzle in a pub, or plod some bleak malarious grove,
But let me toast my shrunken shanks beside some Yankee stove.

The British people say they "don't believe in stoves, y' know;"
Perchance because we warmed 'em so completely years ago!
They talk of "drahfts" and "stuffiness" and "ill effects of heat,"
As they chatter in their barny rooms or shiver 'round the street;
With sunshine such a rarity, and stoves esteemed a sin,
What wonder they are wedded to their fads—catarrh and gin?

In Germany are stoves galore, and yet you seldom find
A fire within the stoves, for German stoves are not that kind;
The Germans say that fires make dirt, and dirt's an odious thing,
But the truth is that the pfennig is the average Teuton's king,
And since the fire costs pfennigs, why, the thrifty soul denies
Himself all heat except what comes with beer and exercise.

The Frenchman builds a fire of cones, the Irishman of peat;
The frugal Dutchman buys a fire when he has need of heat—
That is to say, he pays so much each day to one who brings
The necessary living coals to warm his soup and things;
In Italy and Spain they have no need to heat the house—
'Neath balmy skies the native picks the mandolin and louse.

Now, we've no mouldy catacombs, no feudal castles grim,
No ruined monasteries, no abbeys ghostly dim;
Our ancient history is new, our future's all ahead,
And we've got a tariff bill that's made all Europe sick abed—
But what is best, though short on tombs and academic groves,
We double discount Christendom on sunshine and on stoves.

Dear land of mine! I come to you from months of chill and storm,
Blessing the honest people whose hearts and hearths are warm;
A fairer, sweeter song than this I mean to weave to you
When I've reached my lakeside 'dobe and once get heated through;
But, even then, the burthen of that fairer song shall be
That the land of stoves and sunshine is good enough for me.

A DRINKING SONG

Come, brothers, share the fellowship
We celebrate to-night;
There's grace of song on every lip
And every heart is light!
But first, before our mentor chimes
The hour of jubilee,
Let's drink a health to good old times,
And good times yet to be!
Clink, clink, clink!
Merrily let us drink!
There's store of wealth
And more of health
In every glass, we think.
Clink, clink, clink!
To fellowship we drink!
And from the bowl
No genial soul
In such an hour can shrink.

And you, oh, friends from west and east
And other foreign parts,
Come share the rapture of our feast,
The love of loyal hearts;
And in the wassail that suspends
All matters burthensome,
We'll drink a health to good old friends
And good friends yet to come.
Clink, clink, clink!
To fellowship we drink!
And from the bowl
No genial soul
In such an hour will shrink.
Clink, clink, clink!
Merrily let us drink!
There's fellowship
In every sip
Of friendship's brew, we think.

THE LIMITATIONS OF YOUTH

I'd like to be a cowboy an' ride a fiery hoss
Way out into the big an' boundless west;
I'd kill the bears an' catamounts an' wolves I come across,
An' I'd pluck the bal' head eagle from his nest!
With my pistols at my side,
I would roam the prarers wide,
An' to scalp the savage Injun in his wigwam would I ride—
If I darst; but I darsen't!

I'd like to go to Afriky an' hunt the lions there,
An' the biggest ollyfunts you ever saw!
I would track the fierce gorilla to his equatorial lair,
An' beard the cannybull that eats folks raw!
I'd chase the pizen snakes
An' the 'pottimus that makes
His nest down at the bottom of unfathomable lakes—
If I darst; but I darsen't!

I would I were a pirut to sail the ocean blue,
With a big black flag aflyin' overhead;
I would scour the billowy main with my gallant pirut crew
An' dye the sea a gouty, gory red!
With my cutlass in my hand
On the quarterdeck I'd stand
And to deeds of heroism I'd incite my pirut band—
If I darst; but I darsen't!

And, if I darst, I'd lick my pa for the times that he's licked me!
I'd lick my brother an' my teacher, too!
I'd lick the fellers that call round on sister after tea,
An' I'd keep on lickin' folks till I got through!
You bet! I'd run away
From my lessons to my play,
An' I'd shoo the hens, an' tease the cat, an' kiss the girls all day—
If I darst; but I darsen't!

THE BOW-LEG BOY

Who should come up the road one day
But the doctor-man in his two-wheel shay!
And he whoaed his horse and he cried "Ahoy!
I have brought you folks a bow-leg boy!
Such a cute little boy!
Such a funny little boy!
Such a dear little bow-leg boy!"

He took out his box and he opened it wide,
And there was the bow-leg boy inside!
And when they saw that cunning little mite,
They cried in a chorus expressive of delight:
"What a cute little boy!
What a funny little boy!
What a dear little bow-leg boy!"

Observing a strict geometrical law,
They cut out his panties with a circular saw;
Which gave such a stress to his oval stride
That the people he met invariably cried:
"What a cute little boy!
What a funny little boy!
What a dear little bow-leg boy!"

They gave him a wheel and away he went
Speeding along to his heart's content;
And he sits so straight and he pedals so strong
That the folks all say as he bowls along:
"What a cute little boy!
What a funny little boy!
What a dear little bow-leg boy!"

With his eyes aflame and his cheeks aglow,
He laughs "aha" and he laughs "oho";
And the world is filled and thrilled with the joy
Of that jolly little human, the bow-leg boy—
The cute little boy!

The funny little boy!
The dear little bow-leg boy!

If ever the doctor-man comes my way
With his wonderful box in his two-wheel shay,
I'll ask for the treasure I'd fain possess—
Now, honest Injun! can't you guess?
Why, a cute little boy—
A funny little boy—
A dear little bow-leg boy!

THE STRAW PARLOR

Way up at the top of a big stack of straw
Was the cunningest parlor that ever you saw!
And there could you lie when aweary of play
And gossip or laze in the coziest way;
No matter how careworn or sorry one's mood
No worldly distraction presumed to intrude.
As a refuge from onerous mundane ado
I think I approve of straw parlors, don't you?

A swallow with jewels aflame on her breast
On that straw parlor's ceiling had builded her nest;
And she flew in and out all the happy day long,
And twittered the soothingest lullaby song.
Now some might suppose that that beautiful bird
Performed for her babies the music they heard;
I reckon she twittered her répertoire through
For the folk in the little straw parlor, don't you?

And down from a rafter a spider had hung
Some swings upon which he incessantly swung.
He cut up such didoes—such antics he played
Way up in the air, and was never afraid!
He never made use of his horrid old sting,
But was just upon earth for the fun of the thing!
I deeply regret to observe that so few
Of these good-natured insects are met with, don't you?

And, down in the strawstack, a wee little mite
Of a cricket went chirping by day and by night;
And further down, still, a cunning blue mouse
In a snug little nook of that strawstack kept house!
When the cricket went "chirp," Miss Mousie would squeak
"Come in," and a blush would enkindle her cheek!
She thought—silly girl! 't was a beau come to woo,
But I guess it was only the cricket, don't you?

So the cricket, the mouse, and the motherly bird
Made as soothingsome music as ever you heard
And, meanwhile, that spider by means of his swings
Achieved most astounding gyrations and things!
No wonder the little folk liked what they saw
And loved what they heard in that parlor of straw!
With the mercury up to 102
In the shade, I opine they just sizzled, don't you?

But once there invaded that Eden of straw
The evilest Feline that ever you saw!
She pounced on that cricket with rare promptitude
And she tucked him away where he'd do the most good;
And then, reaching down to the nethermost house,
She deftly expiscated little Miss Mouse!
And, as for the Swallow, she shrieked and withdrew—
I rather admire her discretion, don't you?

Now listen: That evening a cyclone obtained,
And the mortgage was all on that farm that remained!
Barn, strawstack and spider—they all blew away,
And nobody knows where they're at to this day!
And, as for the little straw parlor, I fear
It was wafted clean off this sublunary sphere!
I really incline to a hearty "boo-hoo"
When I think of this tragical ending, don't you?

A PITEOUS PLAINT

I cannot eat my porridge,
I weary of my play;
No longer can I sleep at night,
No longer romp by day!
Though forty pounds was once my weight,
I'm shy of thirty now;
I pine, I wither and I fade
Through love of Martha Clow.

As she rolled by this morning
I heard the nurse girl say:
"She weighs just twenty-seven pounds
And she's one year old to-day."
I threw a kiss that nestled
In the curls upon her brow,
But she never turned to thank me—
That bouncing Martha Clow!

She ought to know I love her,
For I've told her that I do;

And I've brought her nuts and apples,
And sometimes candy, too!
I'd drag her in my little cart
If her mother would allow
That delicate attention
To her daughter, Martha Clow.

O Martha! pretty Martha!
Will you always be so cold?
Will you always be as cruel
As you are at one-year-old?
Must your two-year-old admirer
Pine as hopelessly as now
For a fond reciprocation
Of his love for Martha Clow?

You smile on Bernard Rogers
And on little Harry Knott;
You play with them at peek-a-boo
All in the Waller Lot!
Wildly I gnash my new-cut teeth
And beat my throbbing brow,
When I behold the coquetry
Of heartless Martha Clow!

I cannot eat my porridge,
Nor for my play care I;
Upon the floor and porch and lawn
My toys neglected lie;
But on the air of Halsted street
I breathe this solemn vow:
"Though she be false, I will be true
To pretty Martha Clow!"

THE DISCREET COLLECTOR

Down south there is a curio-shop
Unknown to many men;
Thereat do I intend to stop
When I am south again;
The narrow street through which to go—
Aha! I know it well!
And may be you would like to know—
But no—I will not tell!

'T is there to find the loveliest plates
(The bluest of the blue!)
At such surprisingly low rates
You'd not believe it true!

And there is one Napoleon vase
Of dainty Sèvres to sell—
I'm sure you'd like to know that place—
But no—I will not tell!

Then, too, I know another shop
Has old, old beds for sale,
With lovely testers up on top
Carved in ornate detail;
And there are sideboards rich and rare,
With fronts that proudly swell—
Oh, there are bargains waiting there,
But where I will not tell!

And hark! I know a bottle-man
Smiling and debonair,
And he has promised me I can
Choose of his precious ware!
In age and shape and color, too,
His dainty goods excel—
Aha, my friends, if you but knew—
But no! I will not tell!

A thousand other shops I know
Where bargains can be got—
Where other folk would like to go
Who have what I have not.
I let them hunt; I hold my mouth—
Yes, though I know full well
Where lie the treasures of the south,
I'm not a going to tell!

A VALENTINE

Your gran'ma, in her youth, was quite
As blithe a little maid as you.
And, though her hair is snowy white,
Her eyes still have their maiden blue,
And on her cheeks, as fair as thine,
Methinks a girlish blush would glow
If she recalled the valentine
She got, ah! many years ago.

A valorous youth loved gran'ma then,
And wooed her in that auld lang syne;
And first he told his secret when
He sent the maid that valentine.
No perfumed page nor sheet of gold
Was that first hint of love he sent,

But with the secret gran'pa told—
"I love you"—gran'ma was content.

Go, ask your gran'ma, if you will,
If—though her head be bowed and gray—
If—though her feeble pulse be chill—
True love abideth not for aye;
By that quaint portrait on the wall,
That smiles upon her from above,
Methinks your gran'ma can recall
The sweet divinity of love.

Dear Elsie, here's no page of gold—
No sheet embossed with cunning art—
But here's a solemn pledge of old:
"I love you, love, with all my heart."
And if in what I send you here
You read not all of love expressed,
Go—go to gran'ma, Elsie dear,
And she will tell you all the rest!

THE WIND

(THE TALE)

Cometh the Wind from the garden, fragrant and full of sweet singing—
Under my tree where I sit cometh the Wind to confession.

"Out in the garden abides the Queen of the beautiful Roses—
Her do I love and to-night wooed her with passionate singing;
Told I my love in those songs, and answer she gave in her blushes—
She shall be bride of the Wind, and she is the Queen of the Roses!"

"Wind, there is spice in thy breath; thy rapture hath fragrance Sabaean!"

"Straight from my wooing I come—my lips are bedewed with her kisses—
My lips and my song and my heart are drunk with the rapture of loving!"

(THE SONG)

The Wind he loveth the red, red Rose,
And he wooeth his love to wed:
Sweet is his song
The Summer long
As he kisseth her lips so red;
And he recketh naught of the ruin wrought
When the Summer of love is sped!

(AGAIN THE TALE)

Cometh the Wind from the garden, bitter with sorrow of winter.

"Wind, is thy love-song forgot? Wherefore thy dread lamentations?"

Sigheth and moaneth the Wind: "Out of the desolate garden
Come I from vigils with ghosts over the grave of the Summer!"

"Thy breath that was fragrant anon with rapture of music and loving,
It grieveth all things with its sting and the frost of its wailing displeasure."

The Wind maketh ever more moan and ever it giveth this answer:
"My heart it is numb with the cold of the love that was born of the Summer—
I come from the garden all white with the wrath and the sorrow of Winter;
I have kissed the low, desolate tomb where my bride in her loveliness lieth
And the voice of the ghost in my heart is the voice that forever outcrieth!"

(AGAIN THE SONG)

The Wind he waileth the red, red Rose
When the Summer of love is sped—
He waileth above
His lifeless love
With her shroud of snow o'erspread—
Crieth such things as a true heart brings
To the grave of its precious dead.

A PARAPHRASE

Our Father who art in heaven, hallowed be Thy name;
Thy Kingdom come, Thy will be done on earth, in Heaven the same;
Give us this day our daily bread, and may our debts to heaven—
As we our earthly debts forgive—by Thee be all forgiven;
When tempted or by evil vexed, restore Thou us again,
And Thine be the Kingdom, the Power, and the Glory, forever and ever; amen.

WITH BRUTUS IN ST. JO

Of all the opry-houses then obtaining in the West
The one which Milton Tootle owned was, by all odds, the best;
Milt, being rich, was much too proud to run the thing alone,
So he hired an "acting manager," a gruff old man named Krone—
A stern, commanding man with piercing eyes and flowing beard,
And his voice assumed a thunderous tone when Jack and I appeared;
He said that Julius Caesar had been billed a week or so,
And would have to have some armies by the time he reached St. Jo!

O happy days, when Tragedy still winged an upward flight,
When actors wore tin helmets and cambric robes at night!
O happy days, when sounded in the public's rapturous ears
The creak of pasteboard armor and the clash of wooden spears!
O happy times for Jack and me and that one other supe
That then and there did constitute the noblest Roman's troop!
With togas, battle axes, shields, we made a dazzling show,
When we were Roman soldiers with Brutus in St. Jo!

We wheeled and filed and double-quicked wherever Brutus led,
The folks applauding what we did as much as what he said;
'T was work, indeed; yet Jack and I were willing to allow
'T was easier following Brutus than following father's plough;
And at each burst of cheering, our valor would increase—
We tramped a thousand miles that night, at fifty cents apiece!
For love of Art—not lust for gold—consumed us years ago,
When we were Roman soldiers with Brutus in St. Jo!

To-day, while walking in the Square, Jack Langrish says to me:
"My friend, the drama nowadays ain't what it used to be!
These farces and these comedies—how feebly they compare
With that mantle of the tragic art which Forrest used to wear!
My soul is warped with bitterness to think that you and I—
Co-heirs to immortality in seasons long gone by—
Now draw a paltry stipend from a Boston comic show,
We, who were Roman soldiers with Brutus in St. Jo!"

And so we talked and so we mused upon the whims of Fate
That had degraded Tragedy from its old, supreme estate;
And duly, at the Morton bar, we stigmatized the age
As sinfully subversive of the interests of the Stage!
For Jack and I were actors in the halcyon, palmy days
Long, long before the Hoyt school of farce became the craze;
Yet, as I now recall it, it was twenty years ago
That we were Roman soldiers with Brutus in St. Jo!

We were by birth descended from a race of farmer kings
Who had done eternal battle with grasshoppers and things;
But the Kansas farms grew tedious—we pined for that delight
We read of in the Clipper in the barber's shop by night!
We would be actors—Jack and I—and so we stole away
From our native spot, Wathena, one dull September day,
And started for Missouri—ah, little did we know
We were going to train as soldiers with Brutus in St. Jo!

Our army numbered three in all—Marc Antony's was four;
Our army hankered after fame, but Marc's was after gore!
And when we reached Philippi, at the outset we were met
With an inartistic gusto I can never quite forget.
For Antony's overwhelming force of thumpers seemed to be
Resolved to do "them Kansas jays"—and that meant Jack and me!

My lips were sealed but that it seems quite proper you should know
That Rome was nowhere in it at Philippi in St. Jo!

I've known the slow-consuming grief and ostentatious pain
Accruing from McKean Buchanan's melancholy Dane;
Away out West I've witnessed Bandmann's peerless hardihood,
With Arthur Cambridge have I wrought where walking was not good;
In every phase of horror have I bravely borne my part,
And even on my uppers have I proudly stood for Art!
And, after all my suffering, it were not hard to show
That I got my allopathic dose with Brutus at St. Jo!

That army fell upon me in a most bewildering rage
And scattered me and mine upon that histrionic stage;
My toga rent, my helmet gone and smashed to smithereens,
They picked me up and hove me through whole centuries of scenes!
I sailed through Christian eras and mediæval gloom
And fell from Arden forest into Juliet's painted tomb!
Oh, yes, I travelled far and fast that night, and I can show
The scars of honest wounds I got with Brutus in St. Jo!

Ah me, old Davenport is gone, of fickle fame forgot,
And Barrett sleeps forever in a much neglected spot;
Fred Warde, the papers tell me, in far woolly western lands
Still flaunts the banner of high Tragic Art at one-night stands;
And Jack and I, in Charley Hoyt's Bostonian dramas wreak
Our vengeance on creation at some eensty dolls per week.
By which you see that public taste has fallen mighty low
Since we fought as Roman soldiers with Brutus in St. Jo!

THE TWO LITTLE SKEEZUCKS

There were two little skeezucks who lived in the isle
Of Boo in a southern sea;
They clambered and rollicked in heathenish style
In the boughs of their cocoanut tree.
They didn't fret much about clothing and such
And they recked not a whit of the ills
That sometimes accrue
From having to do
With tailor and laundry bills.

The two little skeezucks once heard of a Fair
Far off from their native isle,
And they asked of King Fan if they mightn't go there
To take in the sights for awhile.
Now old King Fan
Was a good-natured man
(As good-natured monarchs go),

And howbeit he swore that all Fairs were a bore,
He hadn't the heart to say "No."

So the two little skeezucks sailed off to the Fair
In a great big gum canoe,
And I fancy they had a good time there,
For they tarried a year or two.
And old King Fan at last began
To reckon they'd come to grief,
When glory! one day
They sailed into the bay
To the tune of "Hail to the Chief!"

The two little skeezucks fell down on the sand,
Embracing his majesty's toes,
Till his majesty graciously bade them stand
And salute him nose to nose.
And then quoth he:
"Divulge unto me
What happenings have hapt to you;
And how did they dare to indulge in a Fair
So far from the island of Boo?"

The two little skeezucks assured their king
That what he surmised was true;
That the Fair would have been a different thing
Had it only been held in Boo!
"The folk over there in no wise compare
With the folk of the southern seas;
Why, they comb out their heads
And they sleep in beds
Instead of in caverns and trees!"

The two little skeezucks went on to say
That children (so far as they knew)
Had a much harder time in that land far away
Than here in the island of Boo!
They have to wear clo'es
Which (as every one knows)
Are irksome to primitive laddies,
While, with forks and with spoons, they're denied the sweet boons
That accrue from free use of one's paddies!

"And now that you're speaking of things to eat,"
Interrupted the monarch of Boo,
"We beg to inquire if you happened to meet
With a nice missionary or two?"
"No, that we did not; in that curious spot
Where were gathered the fruits of the earth,
Of that special kind
Which Your Nibs has in mind

There appeared a deplorable dearth!"

Then loud laughed that monarch in heathenish mirth
And loud laughed his courtiers, too,
And they cried: "There is elsewhere no land upon earth
So good as our island of Boo!"
And the skeezucks, tho' glad
Of the journey they'd had,
Climbed up in their cocoanut trees,
Where they still may be seen with no shirts to keep clean
Or trousers that bag at the knees.

PAN LIVETH

They told me once that Pan was dead,
And so, in sooth, I thought him;
For vainly where the streamlets led
Through flowery meads I sought him—
Nor in his dewy pasture bed
Nor in the grove I caught him.
"Tell me," 'twas so my clamor ran—
"Tell me, oh, where is Pan?"

But, once, as on my pipe I played
A requiem sad and tender,
Lo, thither came a shepherd-maid—
Full comely she and slender!
I were indeed a churlish blade
With wailings to offend 'er—
For, surely, wooing's sweeter than
A mourning over Pan!

So, presently, whiles I did scan
That shepherd-maiden pretty,
And heard her accents, I began
To pipe a cheerful ditty;
And so, betimes, forgot old Pan
Whose death had waked my pity;
So—so did Love undo the man
Who sought and pined for Pan!

He was not dead! I found him there—
The Pan that I was after!
Caught in that maiden's tangling hair,
Drunk with her song and laughter!
I doubt if there be otherwhere
A merrier god or dafter—
Nay, nor a mortal kindlier than
Is this same dear old Pan!

Beside me, as my pipe I play,
My shepherdess is lying,
While here and there her lambkins stray
As sunny hours go flying;
They look like me—those lambs—they say,
And that I'm not denying!
And for that sturdy, romping clan,
All glory be to Pan!

Pan is not dead, O sweetheart mine!
It is to hear his voices
In every note and every line
Wherein the heart rejoices!
He liveth in that sacred shrine
That Love's first, holiest choice is!
So pipe, my pipe, while still you can,
Sweet songs in praise of Pan!

DR. SAM

TO MISS GRACE KING

Down in the old French quarter,
Just out of Rampart street,
I wend my way
At close of day
Unto the quaint retreat
Where lives the Voodoo Doctor
By some esteemed a sham,
Yet I'll declare there's none elsewhere
So skilled as Doctor Sam
With the claws of a deviled crawfish,
The juice of the prickly prune,
And the quivering dew
From a yarb that grew
In the light of a midnight moon!

I never should have known him
But for the colored folk
That here obtain
And ne'er in vain
That wizard's art invoke;
For when the Eye that's Evil
Would him and his'n damn,
The negro's grief gets quick relief
Of Hoodoo-Doctor Sam.
With the caul of an alligator,
The plume of an unborn loon,

And the poison wrung
From a serpent's tongue
By the light of a midnight moon!

In all neurotic ailments
I hear that he excels,
And he insures
Immediate cures
Of weird, uncanny spells;
The most unruly patient
Gets docile as a lamb
And is freed from ill by the potent skill
Of Hoodoo-Doctor Sam;
Feathers of strangled chickens,
Moss from the dank lagoon,
And plasters wet
With spider sweat
In the light of a midnight moon!

They say when nights are grewsome
And hours are, oh! so late,
Old Sam steals out
And hunts about
For charms that hoodoos hate!
That from the moaning river
And from the haunted glen
He silently brings what eerie things
Give peace to hoodooed men:—
The tongue of a piebald 'possum,
The tooth of a senile 'coon,
The buzzard's breath that smells of death,
And the film that lies
On a lizard's eyes
In the light of a midnight moon!

WINFREDA

(A BALLAD IN THE ANGLO-SAXON TONGUE)

When to the dreary greenwood gloam
Winfreda's husband strode that day,
The fair Winfreda bode at home
To toil the weary time away;
"While thou art gone to hunt," said she,
"I'll brew a goodly sop for thee."

Lo, from a further, gloomy wood,
A hungry wolf all bristling hied
And on the cottage threshold stood

And saw the dame at work inside;
And, as he saw the pleasing sight,
He licked his fangs so sharp and white.

Now when Winfreda saw the beast,
Straight at the grinning wolf she ran,
And, not affrighted in the least,
She hit him with her cooking pan,
And as she thwacked him on the head—
"Scat! scat!" the fair Winfreda said.

The hills gave answer to their din—
The brook in fear beheld the sight.
And all that bloody field within
Wore token of Winfreda's might.
The wolf was very loath to stay—
But, oh! he could not get away.

Winfreda swept him o'er the wold
And choked him till his gums were blue,
And till, beneath her iron hold,
His tongue hung out a yard or two,
And with his hair the riven ground
Was strewn for many leagues around.

They fought a weary time that day,
And seas of purple blood were shed,
Till by Winfreda's cunning lay
That awful wolf all limp and dead;
Winfreda saw him reel and drop—
Then back she went to brewing sop.

So when the husband came at night
From bootless chase, cold, gaunt, and grim,
Great was that Saxon lord's delight
To find the sop dished up for him;
And as he ate, Winfreda told
How she had laid the wolf out cold.

The good Winfreda of those days
Is only "pretty Birdie" now—
Sickly her soul and weak her ways—
And she, to whom we Saxons bow,
Leaps on a bench and screams with fright
If but a mouse creeps into sight.

LYMAN, FREDERICK, AND JIM

(FOR THE FELLOWSHIP CLUB)

Lyman and Frederick and Jim, one day,
Set out in a great big ship—
Steamed to the ocean adown the bay
Out of a New York slip.
"Where are you going and what is your game?"
The people asked those three.
"Darned if we know; but all the same
Happy as larks are we;
And happier still we're going to be!"
Said Lyman
And Frederick
And Jim.

The people laughed "Aha, oho!
Oho, aha!" laughed they;
And while those three went sailing so
Some pirates steered that way.
The pirates they were laughing, too—
The prospect made them glad;
But by the time the job was through
Each of them pirates, bold and bad,
Had been done out of all he had
By Lyman
And Frederick
And Jim.

Days and weeks and months they sped,
Painting that foreign clime
A beautiful, bright vermilion red—
And having a — of a time!
'T was all so gaudy a lark, it seemed
As if it could not be,
And some folks thought it a dream they dreamed
Of sailing that foreign sea,
But I'll identify you these three—
Lyman
And Frederick
And Jim.

Lyman and Frederick are bankers and sich
And Jim is an editor kind;
The first two named are awfully rich
And Jim ain't far behind!
So keep your eyes open and mind your tricks,
Or you are like to be
In quite as much of a Tartar fix
As the pirates that sailed the sea
And monkeyed with the pardners three,
Lyman
And Frederick

And Jim!

BY MY SWEETHEART

Sweetheart, be my sweetheart
When birds are on the wing,
When bee and bud and babbling flood
Bespeak the birth of spring,
Come, sweetheart, be my sweetheart
And wear this posy-ring!

Sweetheart, be my sweetheart
In the mellow golden glow
Of earth aflush with the gracious blush
Which the ripening fields foreshow;
Dear sweetheart, be my sweetheart,
As into the noon we go!

Sweetheart, be my sweetheart
When falls the bounteous year,
When fruit and wine of tree and vine
Give us their harvest cheer;
Oh, sweetheart, be my sweetheart,
For winter it draweth near.

Sweetheart, be my sweetheart
When the year is white and old,
When the fire of youth is spent, forsooth,
And the hand of age is cold;
Yet, sweetheart, be my sweetheart
Till the year of our love be told!

THE PETER-BIRD

Out of the woods by the creek cometh a calling for Peter,
And from the orchard a voice echoes and echoes it over;
Down in the pasture the sheep hear that strange crying for Peter,
Over the meadows that call is aye and forever repeated.
So let me tell you the tale, when, where, and how it all happened,
And, when the story is told, let us pay heed to the lesson.

Once on a time, long ago, lived in the State of Kentucky
One that was reckoned a witch—full of strange spells and devices;
Nightly she wandered the woods, searching for charms voodooistic—
Scorpions, lizards, and herbs, dormice, chameleons, and plantains!
Serpents and caw-caws and bats, screech-owls and crickets and adders—
These were the guides of that witch through the dank deeps of the forest.

Then, with her roots and her herbs, back to her cave in the morning
Ambled that hussy to brew spells of unspeakable evil;
And, when the people awoke, seeing that hillside and valley
Sweltered in swathes as of mist—"Look!" they would whisper in terror—
"Look! the old witch is at work brewing her spells of great evil!"
Then would they pray till the sun, darting his rays through the vapor,
Lifted the smoke from the earth and baffled the witch's intentions.

One of the boys at that time was a certain young person named Peter,
Given too little to work, given too largely to dreaming;
Fonder of books than of chores, you can imagine that Peter
Led a sad life on the farm, causing his parents much trouble.
"Peter!" his mother would call, "the cream is a'ready for churning!"
"Peter!" his father would cry, "go grub at the weeds in the garden!"
So it was "Peter!" all day—calling, reminding, and chiding—
Peter neglected his work; therefore that nagging at Peter!

Peter got hold of some books—how, I'm unable to tell you;
Some have suspected the witch—this is no place for suspicions!
It is sufficient to stick close to the thread of the legend.
Nor is it stated or guessed what was the trend of those volumes;
What thing soever it was—done with a pen and a pencil,
Wrought with a brain, not a hoe—surely 't was hostile to farming!

"Fudge on all readin'!" they quoth; or "that's what's the ruin of Peter!"

So, when the mornings were hot, under the beech or the maple,
Cushioned in grass that was blue, breathing the breath of the blossoms,
Lulled by the hum of the bees, the coo of the ring-doves a-mating,
Peter would frivol his time at reading, or lazing, or dreaming.
"Peter!" his mother would call, "the cream is a'ready for churning!"
"Peter!" his father would cry, "go grub at the weeds in the garden!"
"Peter!" and "Peter!" all day—calling, reminding, and chiding—
Peter neglected his chores; therefore that outcry for Peter;
Therefore the neighbors allowed evil would surely befall him—
Yes, on account of these things, ruin would come upon Peter!

Surely enough, on a time, reading and lazing and dreaming
Wrought the calamitous ill all had predicted for Peter;
For, of a morning in spring when lay the mist in the valleys—
"See," quoth the folk, "how the witch breweth her evil decoctions!
See how the smoke from her fire broodeth on woodland and meadow!
Grant that the sun cometh out to smother the smudge of her caldron!
She hath been forth in the night, full of her spells and devices,
Roaming the marshes and dells for heathenish magical nostrums;
Digging in leaves and at stumps for centipedes, pismires, and spiders,
Grubbing in poisonous pools for hot salamanders and toadstools;
Charming the bats from the flues, snaring the lizards by twilight,
Sucking the scorpion's egg and milking the breast of the adder!"

Peter derided these things held in such faith by the farmer,

Scouted at magic and charms, hooted at Jonahs and hoodoos—
Thinking and reading of books must have unsettled his reason!
"There ain't no witches," he cried; "it isn't smoky, but foggy!
I will go out in the wet—you all can't hender me, nuther!"

Surely enough he went out into the damp of the morning,
Into the smudge that the witch spread over woodland and meadow,
Into the fleecy gray pall brooding on hillside and valley.
Laughing and scoffing, he strode into that hideous vapor;
Just as he said he would do, just as he bantered and threatened,
Ere they could fasten the door, Peter had done gone and done it!
Wasting his time over books, you see, had unsettled his reason—
Soddened his callow young brain with semi-pubescent paresis,
And his neglect of his chores hastened this evil condition.

Out of the woods by the creek cometh a calling for Peter
And from the orchard a voice echoes and echoes it over;
Down in the pasture the sheep hear that shrill crying for Peter,
Up from the spring house the wail stealeth anon like a whisper,
Over the meadows that call is aye and forever repeated.
Such were the voices that whooped wildly and vainly for Peter
Decades and decades ago down in the State of Kentucky—
Such are the voices that cry now from the woodland and meadow,
"Peter—O Peter!" all day, calling, reminding, and chiding—
Taking us back to the time when Peter he done gone and done it!
These are the voices of those left by the boy in the farmhouse
When, with his laughter and scorn, hatless and bootless and sockless,
Clothed in his jeans and his pride, Peter sailed out in the weather,
Broke from the warmth of his home into that fog of the devil,
Into the smoke of that witch brewing her damnable porridge!

Lo, when he vanished from sight, knowing the evil that threatened,
Forth with importunate cries hastened his father and mother.
"Peter!" they shrieked in alarm, "Peter!" and evermore "Peter!"—
Ran from the house to the barn, ran from the barn to the garden,
Ran to the corn-crib anon, then to the smoke-house proceeded;
Henhouse and woodpile they passed, calling and wailing and weeping,
Through the front gate to the road, braving the hideous vapor—
Sought him in lane and on pike, called him in orchard and meadow,
Clamoring "Peter!" in vain, vainly outcrying for Peter.
Joining the search came the rest, brothers and sisters and cousins,
Venting unspeakable fears in pitiful wailing for Peter!
And from the neighboring farms gathered the men and the women,
Who, upon hearing the news, swelled the loud chorus for Peter.

Farmers and hussifs and maids, bosses and field-hands and niggers,
Colonels and jedges galore from cornfields and mint-beds and thickets,
All that had voices to voice, all to those parts appertaining,
Came to engage in the search, gathered and bellowed for Peter.
The Taylors, the Dorseys, the Browns, the Wallers, the Mitchells, the Logans,
The Yenowines, Crittendens, Dukes, the Hickmans, the Hobbses, the Morgans;

The Ormsbys, the Thompsons, the Hikes, the Williamsons, Murrays, and Hardins,

The Beynroths, the Sherleys, the Hokes, the Haldermans, Harneys, and Slaughters—
All, famed in Kentucky of old for prowess prodigious at farming,
Now surged from their prosperous homes to join in that hunt for the truant,
To ascertain where he was at, to help out the chorus for Peter.

Still on those prosperous farms where heirs and assigns of the people
Specified hereinabove and proved by the records of probate—
Still on those farms shall you hear (and still on the turnpikes adjacent)
That pitiful, petulant call, that pleading, expostulant wailing,
That hopeless, monotonous moan, that crooning and droning for Peter.
Some say the witch in her wrath transmogrified all those good people;
That, wakened from slumber that day by the calling and bawling for Peter,
She out of her cave in a thrice, and, waving the foot of a rabbit
(Crossed with the caul of a coon and smeared with the blood of a chicken),
She changed all those folk into birds and shrieked with demoniac venom:
"Fly away over the land, moaning your Peter forever,
Croaking of Peter, the boy who didn't believe there were hoodoos,
Crooning of Peter, the fool who scouted at stories of witches,
Crying of Peter for aye, forever outcalling for Peter!"

This is the story they tell; so in good sooth saith the legend;
As I have told it to you, so tell the folk and the legend.
That it is true I believe, for on the breezes this morning
Come the shrill voices of birds calling and calling for Peter;
Out of the maple and beech glitter the eyes of the wailers,
Peeping and peering for him who formerly lived in these places—
Peter, the heretic lad, lazy and careless and dreaming,
Sorely afflicted with books and with pubescent paresis,
Hating the things of the farm, care of the barn and the garden,
Always neglecting his chores—given to books and to reading,
Which, as all people allow, turn the young person to mischief,
Harden his heart against toil, wean his affections from tillage.

This is the legend of yore told in the state of Kentucky
When in the springtime the birds call from the beeches and maples,
Call from the petulant thorn, call from the acrid persimmon;
When from the woods by the creek and from the pastures and meadows,
When from the spring house and lane and from the mint-bed and orchard,
When from the redbud and gum and from the redolent lilac,
When from the dirt roads and pikes cometh that calling for Peter;
Cometh the dolorous cry, cometh that weird iteration
Of "Peter" and "Peter" for aye, of "Peter" and "Peter" forever!
This is the legend of old, told in the tum-titty meter
Which the great poets prefer, being less labor than rhyming
(My first attempt at the same, my last attempt, too, I reckon!);
Nor have I further to say, for the sad story is ended.

SISTER'S CAKE

I'd not complain of Sister Jane, for she was good and kind,
Combining with rare comeliness distinctive gifts of mind;
Nay, I'll admit it were most fit that, worn by social cares,
She'd crave a change from parlor life to that below the stairs,
And that, eschewing needlework and music, she should take
Herself to the substantial art of manufacturing cake.

At breakfast, then, it would befall that Sister Jane would say:
"Mother, if you have got the things, I'll make some cake to-day!"
Poor mother'd cast a timid glance at father, like as not—
For father hinted sister's cooking cost a frightful lot—
But neither she nor he presumed to signify dissent,
Accepting it for gospel truth that what she wanted went!

No matter what the rest of 'em might chance to have in hand,
The whole machinery of the house came to a sudden stand;
The pots were hustled off the stove, the fire built up anew,
With every damper set just so to heat the oven through;
The kitchen-table was relieved of everything, to make
That ample space which Jane required when she compounded cake.

And, oh! the bustling here and there, the flying to and fro;
The click of forks that whipped the eggs to lather white as snow—
And what a wealth of sugar melted swiftly out of sight—
And butter? Mother said such waste would ruin father, quite!
But Sister Jane preserved a mien no pleading could confound
As she utilized the raisins and the citron by the pound.

Oh, hours of chaos, tumult, heat, vexatious din, and whirl!
Of deep humiliation for the sullen hired-girl;
Of grief for mother, hating to see things wasted so,
And of fortune for that little boy who pined to taste that dough!
It looked so sweet and yellow—sure, to taste it were no sin—
But, oh! how sister scolded if he stuck his finger in!

The chances were as ten to one, before the job was through,
That sister'd think of something else she'd great deal rather do!
So, then, she'd softly steal away, as Arabs in the night,
Leaving the girl and ma to finish up as best they might;
These tactics (artful Sister Jane) enabled her to take
Or shift the credit or the blame of that too-treacherous cake!

And yet, unhappy is the man who has no Sister Jane—
For he who has no sister seems to me to live in vain.
I never had a sister—may be that is why today
I'm wizened and dyspeptic, instead of blithe and gay;
A boy who's only forty should be full of romp and mirth,
But I (because I'm sisterless) am the oldest man on earth!

Had I a little sister—oh, how happy I should be!
I'd never let her cast her eyes on any chap but me;
I'd love her and I'd cherish her for better and for worse—
I'd buy her gowns and bonnets, and sing her praise in verse;
And—yes, what's more and vastly more—I tell you what I'd do:
I'd let her make her wondrous cake, and I would eat it, too!

I have a high opinion of the sisters, as you see—
Another fellow's sister is so very dear to me!
I love to work anear her when she's making over frocks,
When she patches little trousers or darns prosaic socks;
But I draw the line at one thing—yes, I don my hat and take
A three hours' walk when she is moved to try her hand at cake!

ABU MIDJAN

When Father Time swings round his scythe,
Intomb me 'neath the bounteous vine,
So that its juices, red and blithe,
May cheer these thirsty bones of mine.

"Elsewise with tears and bated breath
Should I survey the life to be.
But oh! How should I hail the death
That brings that—vinous grace to me!"

So sung the dauntless Saracen,
Whereat the Prophet-Chief ordains
That, curst of Allah, loathed of men,
The faithless one shall die in chains.

But one vile Christian slave that lay
A prisoner near that prisoner saith:
"God willing, I will plant some day
A vine where liest thou in death."

Lo, over Abu Midjan's grave
With purpling fruit a vine-tree grows;
Where rots the martyred Christian slave
Allah, and only Allah, knows!

ED

Ed was a man that played for keeps, 'nd when he tuk the notion,
You cudn't stop him any more'n a dam 'ud stop the ocean;
For when he tackled to a thing 'nd sot his mind plum to it,
You bet yer boots he done that thing though it broke the bank to do it!

So all us boys uz knowed him best allowed he wuzn't jokin'
When on a Sunday he remarked uz how he'd gin up smokin'.

Now this remark, that Ed let fall, fell, ez I say, on Sunday—
Which is the reason we wuz shocked to see him sail in Monday
A-puffin' at a snipe that sizzled like a Chinese cracker
An' smelt fur all the world like rags instead uv like terbacker;
Recoverin' from our first surprise, us fellows fell to pokin'
A heap uv fun at "folks uz said how they had gin up smokin'."

But Ed—sez he: "I found my work cud not be done without it—
Jes' try the scheme yourselves, my friends, ef any uv you doubt it!
It's hard, I know, upon one's health, but there's a certain beauty
In makin' sackerfices to the stern demands uv duty!
So, wholly in a sperrit uv denial 'nd concession,
I mortify the flesh 'nd smoke for the sake uv my perfession!"

JENNIE

Some men affect a liking
For the prim in face and mind,
And some prefer the striking
And the loud in womankind;
Wee Madge is wooed of many,
And buxom Kate, as well,
And Jennie—charming Jennie—
Ah, Jennie doesn't tell!

What eyes so bright as Daisy's,
And who as Maud so fair?
Who does not sing the praises
Of Lucy's golden hair?
There's Sophie—she is witty,
A very sprite is Nell,
And Susie's, oh, so pretty—
But Jennie doesn't tell!

And now for my confession:
Of all the virtues rare,
I argue that discretion
Doth most beseem the fair.
And though I hear the many
Extol each other belle,
I—I pronounce for Jennie,
For Jennie doesn't tell!

CONTENTMENT

Happy the man that, when his day is done,
Lies down to sleep with nothing of regret—
The battle he has fought may not be won—
The fame he sought be just as fleeting yet;
Folding at last his hands upon his breast,
Happy is he, if hoary and forespent,
He sinks into the last, eternal rest,
Breathing these only works: "I am content."

But happier he, that, while his blood is warm,
See hopes and friendships dead about him lie—
Bares his brave breast to envy's bitter storm,
Nor shuns the poison barbs of calumny;
And 'mid it all, stands sturdy and elate,
Girt only in the armor God hath meant
For him who 'neath the buffetings of fate
Can say to God and man: "I am content."

"GUESS"

There is a certain Yankee phrase
I always have revered,
Yet, somehow, in these modern days,
It's almost disappeared;
It was the usage years ago,
But nowadays it's got
To be regarded coarse and low
To answer: "I guess not!"

The height of fashion called the pink
Affects a British craze—
Prefers "I fancy" or "I think"
To that time-honored phrase;
But here's a Yankee, if you please,
That brands the fashion rot,
And to all heresies like these
He answers, "I—guess not!"—

When Chaucer, Wycliff, and the rest
Express their meaning thus,
I guess, if not the very best,
It's good enough for us!
Why! shall the idioms of our speech
Be banished and forgot
For this vain trash which moderns teach?
Well, no, sir; I guess not!

There's meaning in that homely phrase

No other words express—
No substitute therefor conveys
Such unobtrusive stress.
True Anglo-Saxon speech, it goes
Directly to the spot,
And he who hears it always knows
The worth of "I—guess—not!"

NEW-YEAR'S EVE

Good old days—dear old days
When my heart beat high and bold—
When the things of earth seemed full of life,
And the future a haze of gold!
Oh, merry was I that winter night,
And gleeful our little one's din,
And tender the grace of my darling's face
As we watched the new year in.
But a voice—a spectre's, that mocked at love—
Came out of the yonder hall;
"Tick-tock, tick-tock!" 't was the solemn clock
That ruefully croaked to all.
Yet what knew we of the griefs to be
In the year we longed to greet?
Love—love was the theme of the sweet, sweet dream
I fancied might never fleet!

But the spectre stood in that yonder gloom,
And these were the words it spake,
"Tick-tock, tick-tock"—and they seemed to mock
A heart about to break.

'T is new-year's eve, and again I watch
In the old familiar place,
And I'm thinking again of that old time when
I looked on a dear one's face.
Never a little one hugs my knee
And I hear no gleeful shout—
I am sitting alone by the old hearthstone,
Watching the old year out.
But I welcome the voice in yonder gloom
That solemnly calls to me:
"Tick-tock, tick-tock!"—for so the clock
Tells of a life to be;
"Tick-tock, tick-tock!"-'tis so the clock
Tells of eternity.

OLD SPANISH SONG

I'm thinking of the wooing
That won my maiden heart
When he—he came pursuing
A love unused to art.
Into the drowsy river
The moon transported flung
Her soul that seemed to quiver
With the songs my lover sung.
And the stars in rapture twinkled
On the slumbrous world below—
You see that, old and wrinkled,
I'm not forgetful—no!

He still should be repeating
The vows he uttered then—
Alas! the years, though fleeting,
Are truer yet than men!
The summer moonlight glistens
In the favorite trysting spot
Where the river ever listens
For a song it heareth not.
And I, whose head is sprinkled
With time's benumbing snow,
I languish, old and wrinkled,
But not forgetful—no!

What though he elsewhere turneth
To beauty strangely bold?
Still in my bosom burneth
The tender fire of old;
And the words of love he told me
And the songs he sung me then
Come crowding to uphold me,
And I live my youth again!
For when love's feet have tinkled
On the pathway women go,
Though one be old and wrinkled,
She's not forgetful—no!

THE BROKEN RING

To the willows of the brookside
The mill wheel sings to-day—
Sings and weeps,
As the brooklet creeps
Wondering on its way;
And here is the ring she gave me

With love's sweet promise then—
It hath burst apart
Like the trusting heart
That may never be soothed again!

Oh, I would be a minstrel
To wander far and wide,
Weaving in song the merciless wrong
Done by a perjured bride!
Or I would be a soldier,
To seek in the bloody fray
What gifts of fate can compensate
For the pangs I suffer to-day!

Yet may this aching bosom,
By bitter sorrow crushed,
Be still and cold
In the churchyard mould
Ere thy sweet voice be hushed;
So sing, sing on forever,
O wheel of the brookside mill,
For you mind me again
Of the old time when
I felt love's gracious thrill.

IN PRAISE OF CONTENTMENT

(HORACE'S ODES, III, I)

I hate the common, vulgar herd!
Away they scamper when I "booh" 'em!
But pretty girls and nice young men
Observe a proper silence when
I chose to sing my lyrics to 'em.

The kings of earth, whose fleeting pow'r
Excites our homage and our wonder,
Are precious small beside old Jove,
The father of us all, who drove
The giants out of sight, by thunder!

This man loves farming, that man law,
While this one follows pathways martial—
What moots it whither mortals turn?
Grim fate from her mysterious urn
Doles out the lots with hand impartial.

Nor sumptuous feasts nor studied sports
Delight the heart by care tormented;

The mightiest monarch knoweth not
The peace that to the lowly cot
Sleep bringeth to the swain contented.

On him untouched of discontent
Care sits as lightly as a feather;
He doesn't growl about the crops,
Or worry when the market drops,
Or fret about the changeful weather.

Not so with him who, rich in fact,
Still seeks his fortune to redouble;
Though dig he deep or build he high,
Those scourges twain shall lurk anigh—
Relentless Care, relentless Trouble!

If neither palaces nor robes
Nor unguents nor expensive toddy
Insure Contentment's soothing bliss,
Why should I build an edifice
Where Envy comes to fret a body?

Nay, I'd not share your sumptuous cheer,
But rather sup my rustic pottage,
While that sweet boon the gods bestow—
The peace your mansions cannot know—
Blesseth my lowly Sabine cottage.

THE BALLAD OF THE TAYLOR PUP

Now lithe and listen, gentles all,
Now lithe ye all and hark
Unto a ballad I shall sing
About Buena Park.

Of all the wonders happening there
The strangest hap befell
Upon a famous Aprile morn,
As I you now shall tell.

It is about the Taylor pup
And of his mistress eke
And of the prankish time they had
That I am fain to speak.

FITTE THE FIRST

The pup was of as noble mien

As e'er you gazed upon;
They called his mother Lady
And his father was a Don.

And both his mother and his sire
Were of the race Bernard—
The family famed in histories
And hymned of every bard.

His form was of exuberant mold,
Long, slim, and loose of joints;
There never yet was pointer-dog
So full as he of points.

His hair was like to yellow fleece,
His eyes were black and kind,
And like a nodding, gilded plume
His tail stuck up behind.

His bark was very, very fierce,
And fierce his appetite,
Yet was it only things to eat
That he was prone to bite.

But in that one particular
He was so passing true
That never did he quit a meal
Until he had got through.

Potatoes, biscuits, mush or hash,
Joint, chop, or chicken limb—
So long as it was edible,
'T was all the same to him!

And frequently when Hunger's pangs
Assailed that callow pup,
He masticated boots and gloves
Or chewed a door-mat up.

So was he much beholden of
The folk that him did keep;
They loved him when he was awake
And better still asleep.

FITTE THE SECOND

Now once his master, lingering o'er
His breakfast coffee-cup,
Observed unto his doting spouse:
"You ought to wash the pup!"

"That shall I do this very day",
His doting spouse replied;
"You will not know the pretty thing
When he is washed and dried.

"But tell me, dear, before you go
Unto your daily work,
Shall I use Ivory soap on him,
Or Colgate, Pears' or Kirk?"

"Odzooks, it matters not a whit—
They all are good to use!
Take Pearline, if it pleases you—
Sapolio, if you choose!

"Take any soap, but take the pup
And also water take,
And mix the three discreetly up
Till they a lather make.

"Then mixing these constituent parts,
Let Nature take her way,"
With which advice that sapient sir
Had nothing more to say.

Then fared he to his daily toil
All in the Board of Trade,
While Mistress Taylor for that bath
Due preparation made.

FITTE THE THIRD

She whistled gayly to the pup
And called him by his name,
And presently the guileless thing
All unsuspecting came.

But when she shut the bath-room door,
And caught him as catch-can,
And hove him in that odious tub,
His sorrows then began.

How did that callow, yallow thing
Regret that Aprile morn—
Alas! how bitterly he rued
The day that he was born!

Twice and again, but all in vain
He lifted up his wail;

His voice was all the pup could lift,
For thereby hangs this tale.

'Twas by that tail she held him down,
And presently she spread
The creamy lather on his back,
His stomach, and his head.

His ears hung down in sorry wise,
His eyes were, oh! so sad—
He looked as though he just had lost
The only friend he had.

And higher yet the water rose,
The lather still increased,
And sadder still the countenance
Of that poor martyred beast!

Yet all the time his mistress spoke
Such artful words of cheer
As "Oh, how nice!" and "Oh, how clean!"
And "There's a patient dear!"

At last the trial had an end,
At last the pup was free;
She threw aside the bath-room door—
"Now get you gone!" quoth she.

FITTE THE FOURTH

Then from that tub and from that room
He gat with vast ado;
At every hop he gave a shake,
And—how the water flew!

He paddled down the winding stairs
And to the parlor hied,
Dispensing pools of foamy suds
And slop on every side.

Upon the carpet then he rolled
And brushed against the wall,
And, horror! whisked his lathery sides
On overcoat and shawl.

Attracted by the dreadful din,
His mistress came below—
Who, who can speak her wonderment—
Who, who can paint her woe!

Great smears of soap were here and there—
Her startled vision met
With blobs of lather everywhere,
And everything was wet!

Then Mrs. Taylor gave a shriek
Like one about to die:
"Get out—get out, and don't you dare
Come in till you are dry!"

With that she opened wide the door
And waved the critter through;
Out in the circumambient air
With grateful yelps he flew.

FITTE THE FIFTH

He whisked into the dusty street
And to the Waller lot,
Where bonnie Annie Evans played
With charming Sissy Knott.

And with those pretty little dears
He mixed himself all up—
Oh, fie upon such boisterous play—
Fie, fie, you naughty pup!

Woe, woe on Annie's India mull,
And Sissy's blue percale!
One got that pup's belathered flanks,
And one his soapy tail!

Forth to the rescue of those maids
Rushed gallant Willie Clow;
His panties they were white and clean—
Where are those panties now?

Where is the nicely laundered shirt
That Kendall Evans wore,
And Robbie James' tricot coat
All buttoned up before?

The leaven, which, as we are told,
Leavens a monstrous lump,
Hath far less reaching qualities
Than a wet pup on the jump.

This way and that he swung and swayed,
He gambolled far and near,
And everywhere he thrust himself

He left a soapy smear.

FITTE THE SIXTH

That noon a dozen little dears
Were spanked and put to bed
With naught to stay their appetites
But cheerless crusts of bread.

That noon a dozen hired girls
Washed out each gown and shirt
Which that exuberant Taylor pup
Had frescoed o'er with dirt.

That whole day long the Aprile sun
Smiled sweetly from above
On clotheslines flaunting to the breeze
The emblems mothers love.

That whole day long the Taylor pup
This way and that did hie
Upon his mad, erratic course,
Intent on getting dry.

That night when Mr. Taylor came
His vesper meal to eat,
He uttered things my pious pen
Would liefer not repeat.

Yet still that noble Taylor pup
Survives to romp and bark
And stumble over folks and things
In fair Buena Park.

Good sooth, I wot he should be called
Buena's favorite son
Who's sired of such a noble sire
And dammed by every one!

AFTER READING TROLLOPE'S HISTORY OF FLORENCE

My books are on their shelves again
And clouds lie low with mist and rain.
Afar the Arno murmurs low
The tale of fields of melting snow.
List to the bells of times agone
The while I wait me for the dawn.

Beneath great Giotto's Campanile
The gray ghosts throng; their whispers steal
From poets' bosoms long since dust;
They ask me now to go. I trust
Their fleeter footsteps where again
They come at night and live as men.

The rain falls on Ghiberti's gates;
The big drops hang on purple dates;
And yet beneath the ilex-shades—
Dear trysting-place for boys and maids—
There comes a form from days of old,
With Beatrice's hair of gold.

The breath of lands or lilied streams
Floats through the fabric of my dreams;
And yonder from the hills of song,
Where psalmists brood and prophets throng,
The lone, majestic Dante leads
His love across the blooming meads.

Along the almond walks I tread
And greet the figures of the dead.
Mirandula walks here with him
Who lived with gods and seraphim;
Yet where Colonna's fair feet go
There passes Michael Angelo.

In Rome or Florence, still with her
Stands lone and grand her worshipper.
In Leonardo's brain there move
Christ and the children of His love;
And Raphael is touching now,
For the last time, an angel's brow.

Angelico is praying yet
Where lives no pang of man's regret,
And, mixing tears and prayers within
His palette's wealth, absolved from sin,
He dips his brush in hues divine;
San Marco's angel faces shine.

Within Lorenzo's garden green,
Where olives hide their boughs between,
The lovers, as they read betimes
Their love within Petrarca's lines,
Stand near the marbles found at Rome,
Lost shades that search in vain for home.

They pace the paths along the stream,
Dark Vallombrosa in their dream.

They sing, amidst the rain-drenched pines,
Of Tuscan gold that ruddier shines
Behind a saint's auroral face
That shows e'en yet the master's trace.

But lo, within the walls of gray,
E're yet there falls a glint of day,
And far without, from hill to vale,
Where honey-hearted nightingale
Or meads of pale anemones
Make sweet the coming morning breeze—

I hear a voice, of prophet tone,
A voice of doom, like his alone
That once in Gadara was heard;
The old walls trembled—lo, the bird
Has ceased to sing, and yonder waits
Lorenzo at his palace gates.

Some Romola in passing by
Turns toward the ruler, and his sigh
Wanders amidst the myrtle bowers
Or o'er the city's mantled towers,
For she is Florence! "Wilt thou hear
San Marco's prophet? Doom is near."

"Her liberties," he cries, "restore!
This much for Florence—yea, and more
To men and God!" The days are gone;
And in an hour of perfect dawn
I stand beneath the cypress trees
That shiver still with words like these.

A LULLABY

The stars are twinkling in the skies,
The earth is lost in slumbers deep;
So hush, my sweet, and close thine eyes,
And let me lull thy soul to sleep.
Compose thy dimpled hands to rest,
And like a little birdling lie
Secure within thy cozy nest
Upon my loving mother breast,
And slumber to my lullaby,
So hushaby—O hushaby.

The moon is singing to a star
The little song I sing to you;
The father sun has strayed afar,

As baby's sire is straying too.
And so the loving mother moon
Sings to the little star on high;
And as she sings, her gentle tune
Is borne to me, and thus I croon
For thee, my sweet, that lullaby
Of hushaby—O hushaby.

There is a little one asleep
That does not hear his mother's song;
But angel watchers—as I weep—
Surround his grave the night-tide long.
And as I sing, my sweet, to you,
Oh, would the lullaby I sing—
The same sweet lullaby he knew
While slumb'ring on this bosom too—
Were borne to him on angel's wing!
So hushaby—O hushaby.

"THE OLD HOMESTEAD"

Jest as atween the awk'ard lines a hand we love has penn'd
Appears a meanin' hid from other eyes,
So, in your simple, homespun art, old honest Yankee friend,
A power o' tearful, sweet seggestion lies.
We see it all—the pictur' that our mem'ries hold so dear—
The homestead in New England far away,
An' the vision is so nat'ral-like we almost seem to hear
The voices that were heshed but yesterday.

Ah, who'd ha' thought the music of that distant childhood time
Would sleep through all the changeful, bitter years
To waken into melodies like Chris'mas bells a-chime
An' to claim the ready tribute of our tears!
Why, the robins in the maples an' the blackbirds round the pond,
The crickets an' the locusts in the leaves,
The brook that chased the trout adown the hillside just beyond,
An' the swallers in their nests beneath the eaves—
They all come troopin' back with you, dear Uncle Josh, to-day,
An' they seem to sing with all the joyous zest
Of the days when we were Yankee boys an' Yankee girls at play,
With nary thought of "livin' way out West"!

God bless ye, Denman Thomps'n, for the good y' do our hearts,
With this music an' these memories o' youth—
God bless ye for the faculty that tops all human arts,
The good ol' Yankee faculty of Truth!

CHRISTMAS HYMN

Sing, Christmas bells!
Say to the earth this is the morn
Whereon our Saviour-King is born;
Sing to all men—the bond, the free,
The rich, the poor, the high, the low—
The little child that sports in glee—
The aged folk that tottering go—
Proclaim the morn
That Christ is born,
That saveth them and saveth me!

Sing, angel host!
Sing of the star that God has placed
Above the manger in the east;
Sing of the glories of the night,
The virgin's sweet humility,
The Babe with kingly robes bedight—
Sing to all men where'er they be
This Christmas morn,
For Christ is born,
That saveth them and saveth me!

Sing, sons of earth!
O ransomed seed of Adam, sing!
God liveth, and we have a King!
The curse is gone, the bond are free—
By Bethlehem's star that brightly beamed,
By all the heavenly signs that be,
We know that Israel is redeemed—
That on this morn
The Christ is born
That saveth you and saveth me!

Sing, O my heart!
Sing thou in rapture this dear morn
Whereon the blessed Prince is born!
And as thy songs shall be of love,
So let my deeds be charity—
By the dear Lord that reigns above,
By Him that died upon the tree,
By this fair morn
Whereon is born
The Christ that saveth all and me!

A PARAPHRASE OF HEINE

There fell a star from realms above—
A glittering, glorious star to see!
Methought it was the star of love,
So sweetly it illumined me.

And from the apple branches fell
Blossoms and leaves that time in June;
The wanton breezes wooed them well
With soft caress and amorous tune.

The white swan proudly sailed along
And vied her beauty with her note—
The river, jealous of her song,
Threw up its arms to clasp her throat.

But now—oh, now the dream is past—
The blossoms and the leaves are dead,
The swan's sweet song is hushed at last,
And not a star burns overhead.

THE CONVALESCENT GRIPSTER

The gods let slip that fiendish grip
Upon me last week Sunday—
No fiercer storm than racked my form
E'er swept the Bay of Fundy;
But now, good-by
To drugs, say I—
Good-by to gnawing sorrow;
I am up to-day,
And, whoop, hooray!
I'm going out to-morrow!

What aches and pain in bones and brain
I had I need not mention;
It seemed to me such pangs must be
Old Satan's own invention;
Albeit I
Was sure I'd die,
The doctor reassured me—
And, true enough,
With his vile stuff,
He ultimately cured me.

As there I lay in bed all day,
How fair outside looked to me!
A smile so mild old Nature smiled

It seemed to warm clean through me.
In chastened mood
The scene I viewed,
Inventing, sadly solus,
Fantastic rhymes
Between the times
I had to take a bolus.

Of quinine slugs and other drugs
I guess I took a million—
Such drugs as serve to set each nerve
To dancing a cotillon;
The doctors say
The only way
To rout the grip instanter
Is to pour in
All kinds of sin—
Similibus curantur!

'Twas hard; and yet I'll soon forget
Those ills and cures distressing;
One's future lies 'neath gorgeous skies
When one is convalescing!
So now, good-by
To drugs say I—
Good-by, thou phantom Sorrow!
I am up to-day,
And, whoop, hooray!
I'm going out to-morrow.

THE SLEEPING CHILD

My baby slept—how calm his rest,
As o'er his handsome face a smile
Like that of angel flitted, while
He lay so still upon my breast!

My baby slept—his baby head
Lay all unkiss'd 'neath pall and shroud:
I did not weep or cry aloud—
I only wished I, too, were dead!

My baby sleeps—a tiny mound,
All covered by the little flowers,
Woos me in all my waking hours,
Down in the quiet burying-ground.

And when I sleep I seem to be
With baby in another land—

I take his little baby hand—
He smiles and sings sweet songs to me.

Sleep on, O baby, while I keep
My vigils till this day be passed!
Then shall I, too, lie down at last,
And with my baby darling sleep.

THE TWO COFFINS

In yonder old cathedral
Two lovely coffins lie;
In one, the head of the state lies dead,
And a singer sleeps hard by.

Once had that King great power
And proudly ruled the land—
His crown e'en now is on his brow
And his sword is in his hand.

How sweetly sleeps the singer
With calmly folded eyes,
And on the breast of the bard at rest
The harp that he sounded lies.

The castle walls are falling
And war distracts the land,
But the sword leaps not from that mildewed spot
There in that dead king's hand.

But with every grace of nature
There seems to float along—
To cheer again the hearts of men
The singer's deathless song.

CLARE MARKET

In the market of Clare, so cheery the glare
Of the shops and the booths of the tradespeople there;
That I take a delight on a Saturday night
In walking that way and in viewing the sight.
For it's here that one sees all the objects that please—
New patterns in silk and old patterns in cheese,
For the girls pretty toys, rude alarums for boys,
And baubles galore while discretion enjoys—
But here I forbear, for I really despair
Of naming the wealth of the market of Clare.

A rich man comes down from the elegant town
And looks at it all with an ominous frown;
He seems to despise the grandiloquent cries
Of the vender proclaiming his puddings and pies;
And sniffing he goes through the lanes that disclose
Much cause for disgust to his sensitive nose;
And free of the crowd, he admits he is proud
That elsewhere in London this thing's not allowed;
He has seen nothing there but filth everywhere,
And he's glad to get out of the market of Clare.

But the child that has come from the gloom of the slum
Is charmed by the magic of dazzle and hum;
He feasts his big eyes on the cakes and the pies,
And they seem to grow green and protrude with surprise
At the goodies they vend and the toys without end—
And it's oh! if he had but a penny to spend!
But alas, he must gaze in a hopeless amaze
At treasures that glitter and torches that blaze—
What sense of despair in this world can compare
With that of the waif in the market of Clare?

So, on Saturday night, when my custom invites
A stroll in old London for curious sights,
I am likely to stray by a devious way
Where goodies are spread in a motley array,
The things which some eyes would appear to despise
Impress me as pathos in homely disguise,
And my battered waif-friend shall have pennies to spend,
So long as I've got 'em (or chums that will lend);
And the urchin shall share in my joy and declare
That there's beauty and good in the market of Clare.

A DREAM OF SUNSHINE

I'm weary of this weather and I hanker for the ways
Which people read of in the psalms and preachers paraphrase—
The grassy fields, the leafy woods, the banks where I can lie
And listen to the music of the brook that flutters by,
Or, by the pond out yonder, hear the redwing blackbird's call
Where he makes believe he has a nest, but hasn't one at all;
And by my side should be a friend—a trusty, genial friend,
With plenteous store of tales galore and natural leaf to lend;
Oh, how I pine and hanker for the gracious boon of spring—
For then I'm going a-fishing with John Lyle King!

How like to pigmies will appear creation, as we float
Upon the bosom of the tide in a three-by-thirteen boat—

Forgotten all vexations and all vanities shall be,
As we cast our cares to windward and our anchor to the lee;
Anon the minnow-bucket will emit batrachian sobs,
And the devil's darning-needles shall come wooing of our bobs;
The sun shall kiss our noses and the breezes toss our hair
(This latter metaphoric—we've no fimbriae to spare!);
And I—transported by the bliss—shan't do a plaguey thing
But cut the bait and string the fish for John Lyle King!

Or, if I angle, it will be for bullheads and the like,
While he shall fish for gamey bass, for pickerel, and for pike;
I really do not care a rap for all the fish that swim—
But it's worth the wealth of Indies just to be along with him
In grassy fields, in leafy woods, beside the water-brooks,
And hear him tell of things he's seen or read of in his books—
To hear the sweet philosophy that trickles in and out
The while he is discoursing of the things we talk about;
A fountain-head refreshing—a clear, perennial spring
Is the genial conversation of John Lyle King!

Should varying winds or shifting tides redound to our despite—
In other words, should we return all bootless home at night,
I'd back him up in anything he had a mind to say
Of mighty bass he'd left behind or lost upon the way;
I'd nod assent to every yarn involving piscine game—
I'd cross my heart and make my affidavit to the same;
For what is friendship but a scheme to help a fellow out—
And what a paltry fish or two to make such bones about!
Nay, Sentiment a mantle of sweet charity would fling
O'er perjuries committed for John Lyle King.

At night, when as the camp-fire cast a ruddy, genial flame,
He'd bring his tuneful fiddle out and play upon the same;
No diabolic engine this—no instrument of sin—
No relative at all to that lewd toy, the violin!
But a godly hoosier fiddle—a quaint archaic thing
Full of all the proper melodies our grandmas used to sing;
With "Bonnie Doon," and "Nellie Gray," and "Sitting on the Stile,"
"The Heart Bowed Down," the "White Cockade," and "Charming Annie Lisle"
Our hearts would echo and the sombre empyrean ring
Beneath the wizard sorcery of John Lyle King.

The subsequent proceedings should interest me no more—
Wrapped in a woolen blanket should I calmly dream and snore;
The finny game that swims by day is my supreme delight—
And not the scaly game that flies in darkness of the night!
Let those who are so minded pursue this latter game
But not repine if they should lose a boodle in the same;
For an example to you all one paragon should serve—
He towers a very monument to valor and to nerve;
No bob-tail flush, no nine-spot high, no measly pair can wring

A groan of desperation from John Lyle King!

A truce to badinage—I hope far distant is the day
When from these scenes terrestrial our friend shall pass away!
We like to hear his cheery voice uplifted in the land,
To see his calm, benignant face, to grasp his honest hand;
We like him for his learning, his sincerity, his truth,
His gallantry to woman and his kindliness to youth,
For the lenience of his nature, for the vigor of his mind,
For the fulness of that charity he bears to all mankind—
That's why we folks who know him best so reverently cling
(And that is why I pen these lines) to John Lyle King.

And now adieu, a fond adieu to thee, O muse of rhyme—
I do remand thee to the shades until that happier time
When fields are green, and posies gay are budding everywhere,
And there's a smell of clover bloom upon the vernal air;
When by the pond out yonder the redwing blackbird calls,
And distant hills are wed to Spring in veils of water-falls;
When from his aqueous element the famished pickerel springs
Two hundred feet into the air for butterflies and things—
Then come again, O gracious muse, and teach me how to sing
The glory of a fishing cruise with John Lyle King!

UHLAND'S WHITE STAG

Into the woods three huntsmen came,
Seeking the white stag for their game.

They laid them under a green fir-tree
And slept, and dreamed strange things to see.

FIRST HUNTSMAN
I dreamt I was beating the leafy brush,
When out popped the noble stag—hush, hush!

SECOND HUNTSMAN
As ahead of the clamorous pack he sprang,
I pelted him hard in the hide—piff, bang!

THIRD HUNTSMAN
And as that stag lay dead I blew
On my horn a lusty tir-ril-la-loo!

So speak the three as there they lay
When lo! the white stag sped that way,
Frisked his heels at those huntsmen three,
Then leagues o'er hill and dale was he—
Hush, hush! Piff, bang! Tir-ril-la-loo!

I used to think that luck wuz luck and nuthin' else but luck—
It made no diff'rence how or when or where or why it struck;
But sev'ral years ago I changt my mind, an' now proclaim
That luck's a kind uv science—same as any other game;
It happened out in Denver in the spring uv '80 when
Salty teched a humpback an' win out ten.

Salty wuz a printer in the good ol' Tribune days,
An', natural-like, he fell into the good ol' Tribune ways;
So, every Sunday evenin' he would sit into the game
Which in this crowd uv thoroughbreds I think I need not name;
An' there he'd sit until he rose, an', when he rose, he wore
Invariably less wealth about his person than before.

But once there came a powerful change; one sollum Sunday night
Occurred the tidal wave that put ol' Salty out o' sight.
He win on deuce an' ace an' Jack—he win on king an' queen—
Clif Bell allowed the like uv how he win wuz never seen.
An' how he done it wuz revealed to all us fellers when
He said he teched a humpback to win out ten.

There must be somethin' in it, for he never win afore,
An' when he told the crowd about the humpback, how they swore!
For every sport allows it is a losin' game to luck
Agin the science uv a man who's teched a hump f'r luck;
And there is no denyin' luck wuz nowhere in it when
Salty teched a humpback an' win out ten.

I've had queer dreams an' seen queer things, an' allus tried to do
The thing that luck apparently intended f'r me to;
Cats, funerils, cripples, beggers have I treated with regard,
An' charity subscriptions have hit me powerful hard;
But what's the use uv talkin'? I say, an' say again:
You've got to tech a humpback to win out ten!

So, though I used to think that luck wuz lucky, I'll allow
That luck, for luck, agin a hump aint nowhere in it now!
An' though I can't explain the whys an' wherefores, I maintain
There must be somethin' in it when the tip's so straight an' plain;
For I wuz there an' seen it, an' got full with Salty when
Salty teched a humpback an' win out ten!

Eugene Field was born on 2nd September, 1850 in St. Louis, Missouri at 634 S. Broadway to parents Roswell Martin and Frances Reed Field, both of New England stock. Tragically Field lost his mother at age 6 and was thereafter brought up by a cousin, Mary Field French, in Amherst, Massachusetts.

Field attended Williams College in Williamstown, Massachusetts.

When he was 19 his father died, and Field dropped out of Williams. Field's father, Roswell Martin Field, was the lawyer for Dred Scott, the slave who famously sued for his freedom. The complaint was sometimes referred to as 'The lawsuit that started the Civil War'.

Field then went to Knox College in Galesburg, Illinois, but again dropped out. This time after a year. However he did then summon himself to attend the University of Missouri in Columbia, Missouri, where his brother Roswell was studying. As can be gathered from his efforts to date Field was not the most serious of students but was gaining the reputation of being a prankster. Among his more outlandish attempts were a raid on the president's wine cellar, painting the president's house in school colors, and firing the school's landmark cannons at midnight.

Field tried acting but found it not to his liking, studied law but with little success, but did have an interest in writing for the student newspaper.

When his studies finished in 1871, although he never graduated, he collected his share of his inheritance from his father's estate, and set off for a trip to explore Europe. After six months, with funds from the inheritance exhausted, he returned to the United States.

Field then set to work as a journalist for the St. Joseph Gazette in Saint Joseph, Missouri, in 1875.

That same year he married the sixteen-year-old Julia Sutherland Comstock of St Joseph, Missouri. They would eventually have eight children during their twenty-two years of marriage, of whom only five would reach adulthood. Field, knowing that his understanding of finances was somewhat poor, arranged for all the money he earned to be sent to his wife for her to administer on behalf of the family.

In his career as a journalist he soon found a niche that suited him. His articles were light, humorous and written in a personal and gossipy style that endeared him to his readership. Some were soon being syndicated to other newspapers around the States. Field rose to be the city editor of the Gazette.

From 1876 through 1880, the Family lived in St. Louis. Field worked initially as an editorial writer for the Morning Journal and then for the Times-Journal. From there he worked for a short time as the managing editor of the Kansas City Times before settling, for two years, as the editor of the Denver Tribune. He also wrote a column for the paper, 'Odds and Ends,' poking fun at the climate, the muddy roads, the frontier language, and other aspects of Denver life. However his readership was large and growing. Further opportunities would come.

In 1883 the Field moved the family to Chicago lured by a salary of $50 a week. Field now began work for the Chicago Daily News. Here he wrote his humorous newspaper column called Sharps and Flats. He quickly found out that $50 dollars in Denver didn't stretch that far in bustling Chicago.

His column ran in the newspaper's morning edition. In it Field made quips about issues and personalities of the day, especially regarding the arts and literature. His pet subject was the intellectual superiority of Chicago, especially when he compared it to Boston, which he often did. In

April 1887, he wrote, "While Chicago is humping herself in the interests of literature, art and the sciences, vain old Boston is frivoling away her precious time in an attempted renaissance of the cod fisheries."

In another article that year after Chicago's National League baseball club sold future baseball Hall of Famer Mike "King" Kelly to Boston which overlapped with a speaking tour visit from the famous Boston poet and diplomat James Russell Lowell he wrote: "Chicago feels a special interest in Mr. Lowell at this particular time because he is perhaps the foremost representative of the enterprising and opulent community which within the last week has secured the services of one of Chicago's honored sons for the base-ball season of 1887. The fact that Boston has come to Chicago for the captain of her baseball nine has reinvigorated the bonds of affection between the metropolis of the Bay state and the metropolis of the mighty west; the truth of this will appear in the mighty welcome which our public will give Mr. Lowell next Tuesday."

It was in 1888 that his poem 'Little Boy Blue' was printed in America, a weekly journal. It achieved for Field instant and lasting fame. Coincidentally the same issue carried a poem by James Russell Lowell. Field was immensely pleased that his own poem was regarded with considerably more weight and acclaim.

Field had first published poetry in 1879, when his poem 'Christmas Treasures' was published. It later appeared in 'A Little Book of Western Verse' (1889). This was the beginning that would eventually number over a dozen volumes. He developed a style of light-hearted poems for children. Among the perennial favorites are 'Wynken, Blynken, and Nod' and 'The Duel' (but better known as 'The Gingham Dog and the Calico Cat') and 'Little Boy Blue' about the death of a child. As well as verse Field published an extensive range of short stories including 'The Holy Cross' and 'Daniel and the Devil.'

Field treasured rare, unusual and beautiful books and his personal library had scores of them. He also enjoyed making them too and frequently worked long hours with great care and various colored inks decorating the first letter of his poems.

In 1889 whilst the family were in London and Field himself was recovering from a bout of ill health he wrote his most famous poem; 'Lovers Lane'. It is often thought to have been written whilst the couple were courting but recent research settles it authorship to this later date. The poem was written as a reminder of better days when the couple courted in her father's buggy on 'Lover's Lane, St Jo'.

Field was ever curious and keen to push his boundaries. In 1891 with his brother Roswell they wrote and published 'Echoes from the Sabine Farm' a loosely translated version of Horace.

On 4th November 1895 Eugene Field Sr died in Chicago of a heart attack at the age of 45. He is buried at the Church of the Holy Comforter in Kenilworth, Illinois.

The New York Times described his death: CHICAGO, Nov. 4. — Eugene Field, the poet and humorist, died at 5 o'clock this morning of heart disease at his residence in Buena Park. Although Mr. Field had been ill for the past three days, his sudden death was totally unexpected.

Field was originally interred at Graceland Cemetery in Chicago, but his son-in-law, Senior Warden of the Church of the Holy Comforter, had him reinterred on 7th March, 1926.

Several of his poems were set to music with commercial success. Many of his works were accompanied by paintings from the exceptional talents of Maxfield Parrish.

During his lifetime he was often referred to as the 'poet of childhood'. This may account for his anonymous publication of 'Only a Boy'. In our own times the work would probably be frowned upon. It concerns a 12-year-old boy being seduced by a woman in her 30s. The 1920's drama critic/magazine editor George Jean Nathan claimed it was a popular but forbidden work among those coming of age in the early 1900's.

Much of what Field wrote was light, humourous and of its time. And that is perhaps why it has endured. Its writes of a time that, in his words, suspends itself from the harsh reality of real life to a gentler and more touching time that exists in the imagination.

Eugene Field – A Concise Bibliography

The Tribune Primer (1882)
Culture's Garland (1887)
A Little Book of Profitable Tales (1889)
A Little Book of Western Verse (1889)
With Trumpet and Drum (1892)
Echoes from the Sabine Farm (1893)
The Holy Cross and Other Tales (1893)
Second Book of Verse (1893)
Love Songs of Childhood (1894)
Love Affairs of a Bibliomaniac (1895)
Little Willie (1895)
Songs and Other Verse (1896)
Second Book of Tales (1896)
The House; An Episode in the Lives of Reuben Baker, Astronomer and His Wife Alice (1896)
Field Flowers (1896)
Florence Bardsley's Story (1897)
Lullaby Songs of Childhood (1897)
Lullaby Land (1898)
Sharps and Flats (1900)
The Stars (1901)
Nonsense for Old and Young (1901)
A Little Book of Nonsense (1901)
A Little Book of Tribune Verse (1901)
The Sabine Farm (1903)
John Smith USA (1905)
The Clink of Ice (1905)
Hoosier Lyrics (1905)
Cradle Lullabies (1909)
The Poems of Eugene Field (1910)
Christmas Tales and Christmas Verse (1912)
Penn-Yan Bill's Wooing (1914)
The Yankee Abroad (1917)
The Mouse and the Moonbeam (1919)
Poems of Childhood (1920)

The Gingham Dog and the Calico Cat (1926)
Child Verses (1927)
The Sugar Plum Tree (1929)
In Wink-a-way Land (1930)